The American Indian and the Media

Editorial Staff
Executive Editor, Tim Giago
Managing Editors; Lynne C. Gray, Pamela A. Kalar
Editorial Assistant, Martha Crow
Contributing Editors: Paul O. Sand, Anthony J. Kalar
Original Art and Cover Design, Jacob Castillo
Editorial Consultant, Tom Beaver

Produced as a public service by:
The American Indian Media Image Task Force

Sponsored by:
The National Conference of Christians and Jews,
Minnesota-Dakotas Region

USWEST
FOUNDATION

Star Tribune, Minneapolis-St. Paul

Lerner Publications

Design and printing by Bolger Publications/Creative Printing

Cover Photos: (Clockwise from upper left) Wendell Chino, Walter Echo-Hawk, Wilma Mankiller, Tim Giago and Geraldine Keams.

*"All I have is
my planting stick and my corn.
If you are willing to live
as I do,
you may live here
with me."*

(Instructions given to the ancestors of the present-day Hopi by Maasauu, god of the underworld in charge of the Earth.)

The original art in this book by native artist Jacob Castillo is a contemporary meld of traditional Native American symbols and designs found in the Northwest, Plains, Southwest and other North American indigenous cultures.

All rights reserved under Pan American and International Copyright Conventions

This book is published as a public service. The essays may be used individually for educational purposes without special permission. Wherever possible include a credit line indicating the title of this book and publisher. However, republication or reproduction of any illustration whether it be in a book or in any other material is strictly prohibited without permission in writing from the Publisher.

The republication of this book in whole is prohibited.

Copyright © 1991, by The National Conference of Christians & Jews, Inc.

ISBN 0-9631926-0-4

Library of Congress Catalog Card Number:
91-67943

Acknowledgments

This book had its origins in a three-day conference in April, 1990, the Media and the American Indian, held in Sioux Falls, South Dakota. The conference would have been impossible without the generous support of the Weyerhauser Foundation. In addition, we extend our sincere gratitude to the *Lakota Times, Argus Leader, Rapid City Journal*, and the Sioux Falls Human Relations Commission for making the Conference a great success.

An outcome of the conference was the establishment of the American Indian Media Image Task Force whose major task was to publish a book designed to provide media professionals with a reference for accessing and reporting on American Indians. We are grateful to US West Foundation and to the *Star Tribune* Minneapolis-St. Paul for funding this publication. Our thanks to Lerner Publications for providing the perfect binding. We must also thank our special friend, Patrick J. O'Brien, who has been there for us when we needed him.

This project has enjoyed the energetic, intellectual and artistic input of the members of the American Indian Media Image Task Force and its Advisory Committee who shared their lives and work with us.

Paul O. Sand
Executive Director
National Conference of Christians and Jews
Minnesota-Dakotas Region

Distribution Office:
NCCJ, 100 North Sixth Street, #531-B
Minneapolis, MN 55403
(612) 333-5365

American Indian Media Image Task Force

Jessica Armstrong
Reporter, KESO-TV (CBS), SD

Tom Beaver
NCCJ Director
Member, Muscogee Nation, OK

Kathleen Broyles
National Children's
  Advocacy Center, AL

Margaret Clark-Price
Director of Native
  American Communication
  and Career Development, AZ

Logan Davis
News Director, KEYA, ND

Eugene Fracek
Indian Education Director, SD

Shirley Garnette
Director of Indian
  Education, Rapid City, SD

Gary Garrison
Executive Producer
SD Public Broadcasting

Rhea Gavry
Independent Media Network
Advisor, Sundance Institute, UT

Tim Giago
Publisher/Founder
Lakota Times, SD

Lynne C. Gray
Assistant Director
NCCJ Minnesota-Dakotas

Candy Hamilton
Media Communications
  Program, Oglala Lakota
  College

George Heavy Runner
Blackfeet Tribe, MT

Sylvia Henkin
Chairperson, KSOO Radio, SD

Steven Herman
General Manager, KDLT-TV
  (NBC), SD

Ron Holt
NEA, Leadership
  Communications Specialist
Washington, DC

Geraldine Keams
Navajo Actress, President
  Hozhoni Films, CA

Gary Keller
SD Film Commission

Barry LeBeau
Actor, American Indian Arts, SD

Gemma Lockhart
Writer/Journalist
SD Public Broadcasting

Bonnie London
Lobbyist
SD Legislature

Frank McLeod
Director, Center for
  Indian Studies, Black Hills
  State University

Larry Plank
Blackhills Legal Services, SD

Cynthia Rogers
Minneapolis Public Schools

Paul O. Sand
NCCJ Regional Director
Minnesota-Dakotas

Greg Schnirring
SD Public Radio

Arlene Spiller
Public Communications
NCCJ National Office

Joanna Stancil
Native American
  Communications, Inc.
Washington, DC

Truman Stevens
St. Joseph's School, SD

Rob Swenson
Editor, Argus Leader, SD

Ron Theisz
Professor, Communications
Black Hills State University, SD

Ken Walker
News Director, KSFY-TV
  (ABC), SD

Advisory Committee

Tom Adair
Producer/Director, MN

Rob Armstrong
CBS, Senior Radio
  Correspondent, Washington,
  DC

Paul Augustan
Director/Videographer, MN

Michael Blake
Script Writer, *Dances With
  Wolves*, CA

J. Scott Dodds
Producer/Director, MN

Larry Evers
Editor, Sun Tracks Books
University of Arizona Press

Edie French
Executive Producer, MN

Gus Gustafson
Photographer, MN

Cinda Holt
Director, Sundance Institute, UT

Wilma Mankiller
Principal Chief, Cherokee
  Nation, OK

Chris Spotted Eagle
Producer/Director
Cultural Worker, MN

The National Conference of Christians and Jews
Minnesota-Dakotas Region
Board of Directors

Executive Director:
Paul O. Sand

Assistant Director:
Lynne C. Gray

Edward Baker
Zollie Baratz
Tobin Barrozo
Tom Beaver
Karen M. Bohn
Gladys Brooks
Arthur Caplan
Thomas P. Costello
Dorothy Dolphin
Mischa Dworsky
Nazie M. Eftekhari
Edward Finn
Donald E. Garretson

Tim Giago
Gwen Green
James D. Habiger
Sylvia Henkin
William J. Jaeger, Jr.
Robert N. Katz
Marjorie Loeffler
Earl Miller
James Miller
Roland Minda
Warren Spannaus
Sharron Steinfeldt
Gary Stern
Mary Margaret Tjosvold
Eugene Wise
Marvin Wolfenson

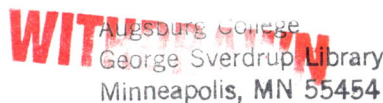
Augsburg College
George Sverdrup Library
Minneapolis, MN 55454

The American Indian and the Media

Introduction	1
Overview on the American Indian by Tim Giago (Nanwica Kciji)	3
Covering Native Americans – *A Non-Indian Reporter's Notebook* by Rob Armstrong	7
Issues to Consider by Pamela A. Kalar	9
Advice from the Inside – *Improving Tribal News Coverage* by Laverne Sheppard	13
Cowboys and Indians by Paul O. Sand	17
Pigskin Mascots: A Seasonal Insult by Tim Giago	21
Tips on Covering and Portraying American Indians by Doris J. Giago and Bill Huntzicker	23
Attack on Sovereignty Relentless by Roger Jourdain	25
"...we really don't trust the media." by Paul O. Sand	28
Positive Images (successes and role models)	31
Resource Directory National Councils — Broadcast Bureau of Indian Affairs — Periodicals State Indian Commissions — Glossary Urban Indian Service Projects — Bibliography Demographics	37

Introduction

"Were it left to me to decide if we should have a government without a newspaper or a newspaper without a government, I should not hesitate a moment to prefer the latter." These words by Thomas Jefferson emblazon the lobbies of newspaper offices coast to coast. But that's only half the story. "The man who never looks into a newspaper is better informed than he who does," Jefferson later wrote, "in as much as he who knows nothing is nearer the truth than he whose mind is filled with falsehood and errors." If America's most outspoken libertarian and the father of the Constitution had problems with the free press of his day, it should be no surprise that others, especially those outside the American mainstream, have also had problems, especially with the pervasive media of this technological age.

Sadly, the earliest images of American Indians in the press were established when they were under siege by the United States government. War machines have always justified their actions by dehumanizing the enemy, the way the Viet Cong were referred to as "Gooks" and "Charlie," but never as "men." Fraternizing with an enemy is strictly forbidden, because disillusionment can open the heart. It's more difficult to kill someone when you've just seen a picture of his wife and children.

Comic books and B-grade movies, lured by the romance of the old West, hungered for consistent, recognizable, and romanticized villains, villains who could be killed without remorse, and the war-time stereotypes endured. When imposed with the new power of Hollywood imagery, they gained unprecedented acceptance. Never has an ethnic group been subjected to a blitz of consistent and unrelenting derogation in the popular media as has the American Indian. Rampaging warriors, drunken bums, subservient *Tontos* and cartoon simpletons are the representations of Indians that America grew up with. Tragically, they are also images that American Indian children grow up with.

Even today, Indians are consistently misjudged and caricatured, in and outside the media, for the very reason that they are different. Their language, dress, religion, behavior, and thought don't fit into any neat pattern easily grasped by mainstream European society, and attempts to do so have lead to misunderstanding and frustration. Indian culture is as diverse as the number of Indian nations, and each nation is as diverse as the number of its members.

Woodward and Burnstein established a legacy of confrontational journalism. In these days of budget cuts and emphasis on profitability, the limited time reporters have for investigation and research is regularly directed at inquisition and expose. Glossy press packets and smooth information agents are too often relied upon to take care of the positive side of balanced reporting. It should be no surprise that American Indians have demonstrated the desire, or perhaps the integrity, to avoid the corporate game of media access. They have often dismissed the mainstream culture in favor of their traditional values.

This book does not attempt to apologize for or advocate Indian causes. Instead, it provides a new perspective on viewing Indian issues, touching on why Indians feel justified in their suspicion of the media, and why true insight into Indian issues often seems elusive to even the most experienced reporter. These impasses can be bridged, with a little knowledge and a fresh, but no less journalistic approach. Sometimes, all it takes is a return to the basics of reportage.

Today, many American Indians feel as though they are again under siege, collateral casualties in a war of fax machines, satellite uplinks, and slick press packages. And therein lies the challenge. Nowhere as in Indian country do journalists need to rely on resourcefulness and skill, instinct and integrity to bring home the real story. Turning the tide of stereotyping and shallow imagery is not an easy undertaking, but it is the kind of pursuit for which most journalists take up pen, word processor, camera or microphone in the first place.

Overview on the American Indian

By Tim Giago (Nanwica Kciji)

The artistic and financial success of Kevin Costner's *Dances with Wolves*, plus the anticipation of the 500th anniversary of Christopher Columbus' errant voyage to the Western Hemisphere, have caused the mainstream media to put American Indians on their agenda in a big way for the first time since the illegal occupation of Wounded Knee, South Dakota in 1973.

All this attention is not necessarily good. When articles written by misinformed journalists serve to perpetuate myths and misconceptions, what purpose do they serve? Most Americans, journalists included, are already ignorant about Native America. Their ignorance is only compounded by half-baked news articles that dwell primarily on the negative.

There are major differences between Indians' view of themselves and the distorted images in the media. Consider this simple fact: "not all of your heroes are our heroes."

George Armstrong Custer is not our hero—obviously. That President Andrew Jackson is not our hero is not so obvious. Andrew Jackson was president of the United States when the Indian Removal Act of 1830 became law. It called for the forced removal of all the tribes in the eastern seaboard states to Oklahoma Territory. It led to what the Indians have called, "The Trail of Tears," a march that left thousands of Indians dead along the way, the American version of the Bataan Death March in the Philippine Islands in World War II.

The next thing to consider is that many events that show the United States government in a bad light, such as the "Trail of Tears," do not appear in the books used to teach the young of this nation about American history.

There are two major reasons that most non-Indian journalists have such a hard time reporting on Indians and Indian tribes. They are unable to consider Indian nations as sovereign, emerging Third World nations within the United States of America, and they are ignorant about treaties.

One of the most elementary and basic rules of journalism is often totally ignored in reporting on Indians and Indian country. The rule as taught in every J-school in the country goes, "If your mother says she loves you, check it out."

Indian nations were sovereign entities long before the advent of the White man. As a matter of record, many of the Indian nations were never militarily defeated. They were forced to surrender because of the deliberate destruction of their economic base. A good example is the destruction of the buffalo herds, which crippled many of the tribes of the Great Plains and eventually forced them to succumb. One must understand that the buffalo was a walking symbol of life to the Plains Indian. It was a spiritual symbol, but equally important to the Plains tribes, this one beast clothed, fed, and housed them. For how many more years would the tribes of the Great Sioux Nation have fought the United States soldiers if the buffalo had not been destroyed?

If the diseases brought to this hemisphere by the White man had not claimed the lives of millions of Indians who had no immunity, would America's history be different?

These basic examples show what happens

when two different cultures collide. The values held by each culture are different. Indians believed in tribal ownership of land, not individual ownership. Goods were often traded between tribes to secure passage across, even the temporary use of, certain lands. Some territories were taken by tribal warfare. The lands were never sold.

The story about Manhattan being sold for $24 in trinkets is a classic example of historical misunderstanding. Most Indian historians believe that, since Indian nations never considered selling land, the tribes involved in the exchange of trinkets for Manhattan really believed that they were only letting the foreigners use the land. The White man never understood this concept and considered the taking of the land a "done deed."

This brief overview is not intended to be a lesson in history as seen through the eyes of the Indian people. It is intended to point out that, owing to cultural differences, extremely differing points of view must be taken into consideration when reporting from Indian country.

Consider that the federal and state governments have created a mishmash of laws affecting Indian people and nations. Some laws differ dramatically from state to state. For example, in some states Indian tribes are affected by Public Law 280, which gives these states law enforcement jurisdiction. But there are other states where Public Law 280 doesn't apply. These states do not have law enforcement or judicial jurisdiction on reservation lands.

In some states like Oklahoma, where more than 100,000 American Indians live, there are no reservations. Then there are states like South Dakota, where Indian lands have clearly defined boundaries and borders, over which the state has absolutely no jurisdiction.

Recently I tried to explain to a black journalist from Nigeria that the Pine Ridge Reservation of South Dakota, the place of my birth, has its own police force, its own highway patrol, its own judiciary, and its own governing body. Since he was never taught such a concept in his study of America, he found it very hard to comprehend.

He did, however, confirm what I have learned from many of the foreign journalists attending school in America, particularly those from nations that had at one time been colonized. He looked at the United States as a land with two faces, a land preaching freedom and justice to the world but unable to fulfill those promises to its own indigenous peoples. He looked upon the American Indians as victims of colonization.

One of the most elementary and basic rules of journalism is often totally ignored in reporting on Indians and Indian country. The rule as taught in every J-school in the country goes, "If your mother says she loves you, check it out."

If someone tells you he or she is Indian and a spokesperson for an organization or a tribe, check it out. Ask them for proof of enrollment in an Indian tribe. It is a simple matter to check their status by calling the enrollment office of the tribe in which they claim membership. When one news chain claimed a large number of Indian employees, I called each one and asked for proof of enrollment. Of the 15 claiming to be Indian, only one was a legally enrolled member of an Indian tribe. If a person applies for a job claiming to be Indian, don't take their word for it. As you would with any claim by a job applicant, check it out.

The other elementary rule of journalism that is often lost when people report on Indians is—be objective. Always remember that there are two sides to every story.

In the past two years major newspapers and television networks have made a practice of seeking out prestigious journalism awards literally over the bodies of the American Indians. A New Mexico newspaper won a Scripps-Howard award for a bloated series on alcoholism among the Navajos, with particular focus on Gallup, New Mexico, a notorious border town. An Alaskan newspaper won a Pulitzer for its windy series on alcoholism among the tribes of Alaska. NBC television news won an Emmy for its terribly one-sided series entitled "A Tragedy at Pine Ridge," a not-so-original report on alcoholism on the Pine Ridge Reservation of South Dakota.

What this proves to me is that readers, and supposed intellectuals who present awards, love to read about or see the misery of other races of people, particularly the First

Americans. Never mind that the other side of the story was never told.

Of course a series of articles on a wonderful man named Gene Thin Elk, who started the Red Road to Recovery movement that is sweeping Indian country, and who is ripping down the walls of alcoholism by addressing the causes through the spiritual eyes of the afflicted, is not news.

When a large tribe like the Cheyenne River Sioux Tribe of South Dakota, a tribe living on a reservation of more than two million acres, passes a resolution to end alcoholism by the year 2000, and passes a law to regulate the sale of all alcoholic beverages within its boundaries, and when it begins to enforce that law by shutting down liquor stores and bars which refuse to purchase tribal liquor and business licenses, it is not national news. Why?

If every journalist would read the following comment, by a letter writer to the Wall Street Journal, and apply it to Indian country, we would be on our way to achieving objective reporting. The writer said "I have always thought that all Americans were free to find their own limitations. It is the freedom to fail that allows the hope of success and without hope anyone is disabled." Until a few years ago, the Indian people were not allowed the freedom to fail. Most of their failures have come at the hands of a paternalistic government.

The fact that the Indian people themselves are addressing their longstanding problems, and are on the way to solving many of them because, for the first time, they are being allowed to do it themselves, is not news.

Print and electronic journalists have played upon the ignorance of their readers when it comes to reporting on Indians, even though, I suspect, they know better. They realize that we are a very small minority and that the repercussions of their inaccurate stories will therefore be miniscule. They believe that they can turn in any article about Indians, no matter how inaccurate, with total impunity. In most cases they are right, because their editors are also ill-equipped to edit their stories.

Nationwide, the media's standard approach is to check the calendar occasionally and then set aside a little time and a reporter or two for a once-in-a-decade, epic Indian series. More likely than not, the epic is a labor to read, and usually it is a rehash of all that is bad in Indian country.

Who is the winner with this type of journalism? The reporting organization? Sometimes they do win large awards. The readers? Not if they are being fed stereotypes; their ignorance is only being extended. Certainly the people of the Indian nations are not the winners—they are probably the biggest losers.

> We are a people who believe in our own sovereignty. We believe we can progress with the rest of America without losing our spirituality, culture, or traditions. Knowing these things, you will be able to approach a news story with more objectivity and a clearer understanding of Native America.

My advice to eager reporters assigned to Indian country is basic and simple: do your homework. Look at these articles as challenges. If you must go to an Indian journalist for leads, don't be so falsely proud that you ignore a knowledgeable source.

And for God's sake, don't find yourself a pet spokesperson. What Indian can speak for hundreds of different Indian nations? That's like finding a European spokesman to talk for all the nations of Europe.

If you are writing about health, find Indian professionals in that field. The same holds true for education, tribal government, justice and on and on. Remember, if you travel to Indian country determined to find the worst, that is exactly what you will find. Don't report on the obvious — broken down cars, winos sitting in alleys — and don't be afraid to use the local tribal government as a source. After all, it is the elected governing body of the tribe.

Never forget that each Indian tribe has its own official spokesperson. Don't bypass that official just because you think he or she might be feeding you tribal propaganda. Reporters attending news conferences for state governors and presidents of the United States are able to cut through the baloney, for the most part. Tribal spokespeople are the same. They are employed by the tribe to give out political information. Take what they say with a grain of salt, but don't ignore them. They can often give you invaluable leads.

In many Indian tribes the children are taught that direct and prolonged eye contact is considered to be very disrespectful. If the person you interview does not make continuous eye contact, that person should not be considered shy or possibly dishonest. It is a matter of cultural differences, nothing more.

This article may not be the media educator I would like it to be because after 20 years of being a media watchdog for the Indian people, I have become a skeptic. But it is a small beginning—and as the old Indian saying goes, "When one sets out on a trip of 100 miles, it always begins with a single step."

In the long run, it is management that will decide whether the non-Indian press continues to report the bureaucratic party line to the detriment of the Indian nations or chooses to put a little elbow grease into the stories that it writes. Hopefully this article will reach into the rarified air of the editors and network moguls of the national media and cause them to assign reporters to Indian country who have the background and training to be knowledgeable and objective.

Educating America about the true history and contemporary face of Indian country will be a monumental task, and it must begin with the media. So far the media has failed this task quite miserably. Keep in mind that Indian America has not been sealed up in a vacuum for the past 200 years. In order to survive, it has progressed, in keeping with its traditions and culture.

Begin with these facts. We are not "your Indians," the vanishing Americans, people still living in teepees. We do not all live on welfare, we do pay taxes, we are not all alcoholics, we do not get a government check every month. We are a people who believe in our own sovereignty. We believe we can progress with the rest of America without losing our spirituality, culture, or traditions. Knowing these things, you will be able to approach a news story with more objectivity and a clearer understanding of Native America.

This article appeared in Nieman Reports-*Summer 1991 and as a 3-part series in the* Lakota Times.

Covering Native Americans – A Non-Indian Reporter's Notebook

By Rob Armstrong

For some reason that is a mystery to me, a lot of news people have the idea that covering stories involving Native Americans is, somehow, different than covering any other story. The fact is that the subject matter is different, but the criteria remain the same: fairness, accuracy, focus, and—of course—the basic who, what, when, where and why.

The job of the reporter is not to know the answers; the job of the reporter is to know the right questions. And therein lies one of the fundamental problems when non-Indian reporters cover Indian stories. In far too many cases, non-Indian newspeople simply have failed to do the basic homework required to ask the right questions.

No reporter worth his or her salt would set out to do a story on, say, the potential benefits of recombinant DNA without doing a little research on gene splicing. But reporters set out routinely to do a story on, say, the uncertain future of the 1868 Fort Laramie Treaty armed with little more than the body of knowledge they obtained by watching *How the West Was Won*.

The unfortunate way in which some non-Indian news organizations have covered Native Americans has set up a pair of parallel circumstances that seem destined to defeat each other. Many Indians feel that they—sometimes individually and certainly collectively—have been victims of biased, unfair and even wrong stories, therefore why help a non-Indian reporter? A lot of non-Indian newspeople have the perception—sometimes a justified perception—that Indians are secretive, tight-lipped and simply don't want news coverage, so why beat my head against a rock? If the cycle is to be broken, both attitudes must change.

I hesitate to present any list of specific suggestions, because such lists are either accepted as gospel or rejected because they are incomplete. Nonetheless, here are a

ROB ARMSTRONG
Armstrong is the Senior Correspondent for CBS News, radio. He is based in Washington, D.C.

few, very basic notions which come to mind and may help.

■ Before you even contemplate writing a story, take a little time to find out something of the culture of the tribe or tribes you may be writing about. (That does not mean go to the library and read some White anthropologist's dissertation; that means find a member of the tribe and have a chat!) A little cultural background enriches every story you write regardless of whether the story itself focuses on economics, crime, education or whatever.

■ Develop your sources, learn who the players are just as you would if you were covering the city council or the state legislature. By learning who the players are you'll come to know who is credible and who is not, who is running for office, who has a special interest, etc.

■ Never assume that because you have one good interview on a given subject that you have a complete story. I have never covered an Indian story that encompassed only one point of view.

■ If you don't know something, ask! Do not go to print or on the air with a piece of information that you simply think is correct. That's how mistakes get made and that's how stereotypes g'et reinforced. Check your facts! (Sound too elementary even to be worth mentioning? Don't bet on it!)

■ Look for more than the easy hit. There is no doubt that Indian America is beset with tremendous problems—alcohol and drug abuse, crime, illiteracy, teenage pregnancy, and on and on. You're not going to win a Pulitzer or a Peabody for doing that story any more than you'll win a prize by doing a story that says "drugs have made Washington, D.C. the nation's murder capital." It's too obvious. Dig a little deeper. If something is working, why is it working? If something is not working, why not?

I have been covering Native Americans and Indian issues since I covered the 1973 occupation of Wounded Knee. I have done all types of stories—stories about successes and stories about failures and stories about good people doing good things and stories about bad people involved in corruption, crime and malice. I have been called some of the names you might expect a White reporter to be called in Indian country. But while I am not the most popular reporter and I am not universally loved among Native Americans, I have never been accused of being unfair in my coverage.

If that is a measure of success, I accept that. Unfortunately, it will only be a beginning until such a time that fairness in covering Native Americans by non-Indian reporters is the norm, not the exception.

Issues to Consider

By Pamela A. Kalar

Contributions

With faces painted with red or black streaks, saddles hidden under blankets, war bonnets blowing in the wind, stereotypical American Indians blaze across the big and little screens massacring settlers. Their contributions to contemporary society are little known and seldom dramatized.

Many necessities and valuable commodities of modern life are directly tied to Indian culture. Herbs used in the medicines of Indian healers are the sources for more than 200 contemporary medicines. Half of today's agricultural products were domestic crops cultivated by Indians, such as white potatoes, rhubarb, tomatoes and corn. Snow goggles, dogsleds, parkas and snowshoes are Indian inventions. Common words, like punk, pee-wee and tuxedo, are derived from native languages. America's highways follow Indian trails, and the asphalt which covers the highway is a substance used by Native nations. High-rise apartment buildings and air-conditioning are designs from the early southwestern nations which have been developed for contemporary use.

Many American rivers, mountains and cities have native names. Twenty-five states' names are derived from Indian names. Alabama, Arkansas, Iowa, Idaho, the Dakotas, and Utah are tribal names.

Thomas Jefferson visited the Iroquois League or League of Five Nations. The governmental structure of this League had such an impact on Jefferson that he incorporated much of what he learned into the Constitution of the United States.

More than stereotypical caricatures and models for dime-store war bonnets and plastic, Hong Kong-produced tom-toms and dolls, the growing living legacy of American Indian peoples is not yet widely recognized.

State name	English meaning	Language
Alaska	mainland	(Aleut)
Arizona	place of the small spring	(Papago)
Connecticut	place of the long river	(Algonquin)
Illinois	men	(Algonquin)
Kansas	people of the south wind	(Sioux)
Kentucky	meadow	(Iroquois)
Massachusetts	the place of large hills	(Algonquin)
Minnesota	cloudy water	(Sioux)
Mississippi	big river	(Algonquin)
Missouri	people of the big canoes	(Algonquin)
Nebraska	flat water	(Sioux)
Ohio	beautiful	(Iroquois)
Oklahoma	red people	(Muskogee)
Tennessee	the name of a Cherokee village	
Texas	friends	(Caddoan)
Wisconsin	the gathering waters	(Algonquin)
Wyoming	on the great plain	(Algonquin)

Their contributions to our contemporary lifeways and mainstream culture are a rich source of topics for this generation's media professionals.

Sovereignty

The legal status of Indian nations is a confused and delicate issue on which volumes have been written. In 19th century treaties while Indian nations were still a very real military threat, the United States Government recognized the sovereignty of Indian nations, yet the United States Supreme Court has referred to these same peoples as "domestic dependent nations" or "wards of the government." The same court gave the United States government title to Indian lands using the Doctrine of Discovery.

The legal status of Indians prior to the 1920s was similar to that of a minor child — their lives were strictly regulated by the government, and they were allowed no input into decisions affecting them. The Indian Reorganization Act of 1934 instituted tribal government under the Bureau of Indian Affairs' scrutiny. In recent decades, laws such as the Indian Education and Self Determination Act have helped to empower Indians and politically strengthen Native national sovereignty.

American Indians were given voting citizenship for the first time in 1924, except in Arizona and New Mexico where it took until 1946. In the 1970s Indian political activism became widespread, leading to demands for change. In recent decades Indians have chosen to fight battles in the courts.

Sovereignty has been under attack for 500 years. Native nations are still fighting to protect their people, land and resources from the encroachment set in motion by Columbus. Genocide, termination, and relocation are some of the weapons that have been used to undermine sovereignty. Contemporary attacks include disputing treaty-granted hunting and fishing rights, and the taxation of government payments for stolen Indian lands. Native lands are being proposed for garbage and nuclear waste dumps while recent legislation, such as the National Indian Gaming Act attempts to pry monies away from Indian nations.

Despite the systematic effort to undermine the sovereignty of modern Indian nations the strength of these unique political entities continues to grow. For a more complete discussion of the complex issue of sovereignty we refer you to *The Nations Within* by Vine Deloria and Clifford Lytle.

Reservation Life

Through policies and practices such as assimilation, allotment, and termination, the United States government has sought to undo the reservations it created, attempting to separate the tribes from their lands and wash its hands of the "Indian problem." Cultural insensitivity, voracious greed, paternalism, and the bitter fruits of inept law-making have compounded the inequities suffered by Native peoples on and off reservations.

Currently, well tended farms, ranches, and homes can be seen on reservations, along with modern community centers, clinics, businesses, and colleges. Although great strides have been made in recent decades, today you will still find tarpaper shacks, log dwellings and dilapidated, cheaply-built federal housing on many reservations. Running water, electricity, reliable heating sources, and safe drinking water are luxuries in the far reaches of some. It is easy for shallow reporting to deepen misunderstandings about such things.

Media audiences have been fed a diet of negative images for 200 years. The resulting cultural bias leads to unthinking negativism and value judgements which are difficult to distinguish from racism. In addition to the obvious woes like alcoholism, poverty, and health problems, reporters are obligated to cover the success stories. Find out what has been accomplished; what is being done to rectify problems; and who is doing it.

Political rhetoric and posturing have done nothing to improve conditions on the reservation. Endless dignitaries have come to smile and gladhand and get pictures of themselves wearing headdresses, then leave. Find out where real positive change is occuring, and why. An understanding of American Indian cultural values, of family and tribal relationships, and of the spiritual and practical importance of the land will enhance the quality of media information and positively influence non-Indian people.

Education

From the late 1800s until the 1960s, church-affiliated boarding schools aided in the government's policy of assimilation. These schools were a nightmare for a half-million Indians. Families were ripped apart, and children were warehoused in cold, barren dormitories. Children were often severely punished for speaking their native languages and observing native customs and ceremonies. Most such church-sponsored schools have been closed.

The Bureau of Indian Affairs also ran a number of boarding schools, and today continues to maintain seven facilities. Today's schools little resemble their predecessors, but generations of Indians still carry the scars of the boarding-school years.

In the 1970s predominantly white schools provided substandard education for Indian children. The drop-out rate for Indian students was twice that of non-Indians. For example, only 35% of those who graduated from high school entered college.

The solution to the education problem is coming from within Indian communities. The nineties have been characterized by a marked increase in the number of Native students graduating from colleges, universities, and technical schools. Contract schools like Little Wounded Knee, on the Pine Ridge Reservation in South Dakota, and colleges like Sinte Gleska College, on South Dakota's Rosebud Reservation, offer Indian-developed curricula implemented by Indian educators, with emphasis on learning their Native languages.

Land and Treaty Rights

To aboriginals worldwide, the land is the source of all life, the Mother. It has fed, clothed, housed and nursed them without great effort and prodigious technology. In return they treat the land and its creatures with great respect. The concept of selling the land is completely alien.

Land is the hub around which most Indian issues revolve. It has been the hub since Europeans first came to the Americas. Over the land we see the clash and spark of two conflicting value systems. From the beginning the land that was rich in obvious natural resources was purchased, connived or stolen from Native Americans.

Most reservations are remnants of the land once agreed to in the treaties. The land is often too barren to pursue agriculture or timber harvesting. Fertile farming or grazing land was sold after allotment, or has been leased to relatively well-to-do non-Indian neighbors.

Tribes were relocated to barren reservations thought to be worthless. Beneath some reservations were hidden resources—first precious metals, then coal, then uranium. Each discovery led to a new wave of land grabbing. In the process, treaties negotiated in good faith have been ignored again and again.

In the second half of this century, American Indians have been asking for the return of land—sacred sites, state and federal land, reservation land stolen by guile—assured by the treaties. For the most part, they have been offered money instead, usually much less than the true "value" of the land, but increasingly, they are refusing. The experiences of allotment and termination have reinforced their traditional belief that without the land, their culture would cease to exist. That would be a great loss, indeed, as the folly of exploitation belatedly dawns on the rest of America.

The once sacred places are now littered with gaudy concessions and mine tailings. To Western culture, alienated from the universe, nature is something to be dominated. Home on the range, seldom was heard a discouraging word. But even in the amiable 80s, "greenhouse effect," "water table shrinkage," "ozone depletion," "acid rain," "toxic waste," and "rain forest depletion," were all media buzz words.

Slowly, it is becoming evident that the aboriginal practice of land stewardship is intensely practical and that it embodies ancient traditional wisdom. Not so long ago this view of the world, along with the religious ritual and culture to which it gave birth, was smugly termed "primitive." Indians are the cultural repository of knowledge about traditional conservation in the Americas.

Contrary to popular belief, not all land was taken from American Indians by fearless cavalry charges and innocent immigrants who had suffered at the hands of the savage red menace. Treaties, ratified by Congress, promised American Indians rights and services in perpetuity in return for the use of tens of millions of acres which were ceded to the U.S. It is astonishing that anyone should expect Indians to willingly relinquish what is left of their once vast homelands, and even more astonishing that few Americans understand why Indians are entitled to exercise treaty rights.

Some states have passed laws that violate the legal terms of treaty rights. Indians attempting to fish in Washington state have been set upon, beaten and jailed by overzealous law officers. For several years, throngs of shouting White sportsmen have threatened Indians exercising spearfishing rights in Wisconsin. Native spearfishing is a reflection of traditional conservation observing self-imposed limits. Indians take only a small percentage of the fish; the great bulk of them are taken by sportsmen. A national overview of contemporary land-related problems as seen by Indian individuals can be found in Vine Deloria's *God is Red* (see bibliography.)

As a result of teachers, textbooks and the media glossing over a shameful history, the average non-Indian in America knows little or nothing about treaty rights. Treaties are legally recognized agreements which should remain time-honored promises.

For more information, treaties are maintained in the Diplomatic, Legal, and Fiscal Records Division, National Archives and Records Service, 8th Street and Pennsylvania Avenue N.W., Washington, D.C. 20408. Photocopies are available for a fee upon request.

Pamela A. Kalar is from the Miami Nation in Indiana. She teaches American Indian literature and composition at Brainerd Community College in Minnesota and is an activist for Indian education.

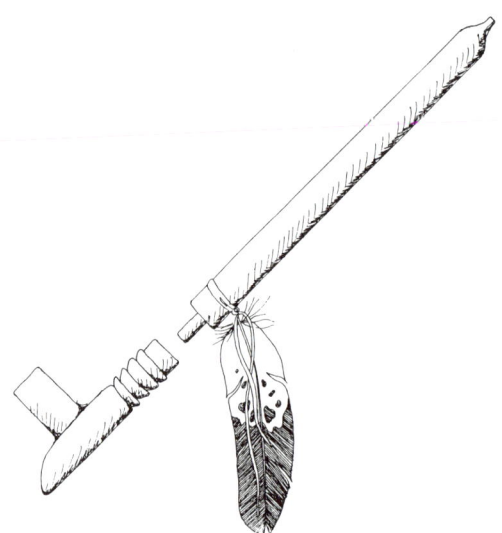

Advice From the Inside – Improving Tribal News Coverage

By Laverne Sheppard

It was the reservation's biggest news story of the year: six local American Indians had just died in a car crash while on a weekend trip to a nearby gambling town. Nearly every family in the community was touched in some way by the deaths. Nearly every family found out about the crash when a story ran the next day in the local off-reservation daily—on page six of the "B" section.

Had the victims been White, would the story have run near the back of the newspaper? Did the editors and police wonder, as the reservation community did, why no money was found on the victims, who had been heading toward a Nevada gambling town?

> ... when news about American Indians is covered only from afar, much of what is human is lost in statistics and stereotypes.

LAVERNE SHEPPARD, Executive Director, Native American Journalists Association
Sheppard is an American Indian journalist from the Fort Hall Reservation in Idaho. She has held editorial positions with *Sho-Ban News*, and *The Bengal*, and was an American Indian/Alaska Native Media Specialist for the United States Census Bureau.

Typically, the weekly tribal newspaper filled the void for the American Indian community. It "humanized" the accident by running an extensive front-page story about the deaths and how they impacted the community. Several weeks later, the tribal newspaper reported the findings of a tribal investigator who, after pouring through police reports and conducting countless interviews, concluded that money had been removed from the victims after the crash. These findings were never reported by the off-reservation media.

The simple act of news placement (or lack of it) speaks volumes about the mainstream media's "usual and accustomed" treatment of Indian news. The daily newspaper referred to above missed several follow-up stories because it didn't have a reporter who regularly covered the reservation—nine miles away. The excuse most media have for not regularly covering Indian communities is that they are too far away from population centers. But when news about American Indians is covered only from afar, much of what is human is lost in statistics and stereotypes. Piecemeal coverage from a distance has contributed to the stereotypes of American Indians as lifeless, emotionless human beings, distraught with alcoholism, unemployment and suicide. The media helped to create this image from their perches on the other side of the border. It's the image which the general public has accepted because it has no first-hand knowledge about these "distant" Indian lands. The mainstream media deserve much of the blame for fueling misconceptions about Native Americans. They have never taken the time to get to know who we are. Yes, Virginia, Indians celebrate Christmas, rake lawns, buy homes and cry at funerals. The general public deserves to know that American Indians are real—not some vanishing part of this nation's past.

The Reservation Revolving Door

During my five years as editor of a tribal newspaper, I met many off-reservation reporters who sincerely wanted to provide fair and accurate coverage of the reservation. But most of these reporters weren't around long enough to achieve it. Media in close proximity to Indian communities have a tendency to turn those communities into training grounds for their up-and-coming journalists. Mainstream media's biggest failure in Indian country is its failure to have a presence there. Seasoned reporters are rarely if ever assigned to regular beats in Indian communities. But there are alternative ways to improve coverage in Indian communities:

■ Assign a reporter to at least a part-time beat in the community. Make sure the reporter has a variety of sources—in the police department, courts, social services, Bureau of Indian Affairs, tribal council, attorney's office, planning and zoning, etc. Reporters should prepare a list of these sources for their organization's future reference, in case they are reassigned.

■ Contact the tribal employment office—usually called the TERO (Tribal Employment Rights Ordinance) or JPTA (Job Training Partnership Act) office—and find out if someone looking for a job may have the skills to become a correspondent. This person may need some training, but he or she could cover everyday news in the community and provide leads on the bigger stories.

■ The tribal education office may be able to suggest a college journalism student who could work part-time or intern over the summer. Who knows, he or she may have what it takes to become a regular reporter, or even an editor.

■ Develop a working relationship with the tribal newspaper, newsletter or radio station. Tribally-funded media often are restricted from covering certain stories, but if you gain their trust they may be willing to pass their leads to you.

The media breed distrust in Indian communities when they remain ignorant of a tribe's unique form of government, its laws, its history and people.

Some Advice from the Inside

My advice to journalists covering Indian communities is this: remember that many of the rules that apply off the reservation don't apply on it. Here are some things to keep in mind.

■ Tribal governments are not bound by open-meeting laws, so if you get kicked out of a meeting, don't raise a big stink. Develop contacts on the tribal council who can tell you what happened. If you develop enough contacts, the council may vote to let you stay in the meeting the next time.

■ Stay away from self-proclaimed "traditional" leaders or experts. In fact, use the word "traditional" with extreme caution. What's tradition for one American Indian may not be tradition for another.

■ Find out what the different tribal factions are (in the mainstream they're known as political parties). Be sure to get views from both sides when covering hot potato stories.

■ Learn as much as you can about the tribe's history, laws and culture. Much of what is happening today in Indian country can be put into perspective by researching the past. If you're on deadline, talk to the tribal historian or librarian, or ask the tribal attorneys. (One of the most glaring mistakes that media make is the use of the phrase "tribe claims to have" when describing tribal laws or treaties affirmed by the nation's highest courts. A run-of-the-mill story about a court decision or tribal council action can easily be slanted by a reporter who, in the back of his or her mind, remains skeptical of the tribe's ability to govern itself and enact its own laws.)

■ Always ask an American Indian how he or she wants to be identified. When in doubt about a person's tribal affiliation, call the tribe's enrollment office.

■ Don't always rely on the same sources for quotes for your stories. The chairperson or president, though oftentimes the designated public spokesperson, does not represent the only view of a particular tribe. Talk to other council members, program directors, people at the store, and the elderly at nutrition program lunch.

■ Make an effort to balance bad stories with good stories. Yes, there are both. If you goof up a story, personally apologize to the affected parties rather than rationalizing your mistake.

■ Be patient. It may take a while to develop the sources you need to cover the real news. Many American Indian communities are hesitant to open up to outsiders because those that preceded you burned the bridges before they left. Prove to them that you're committed to being objective and that you're going to be around for a while.

■ Recognize that problems of unemployment, poverty and substance abuse are not "new." Cover the reasons for such problems (history, culture, laws?) and what's being done to alleviate them.

The media breed distrust in Indian communities when they remain ignorant of a tribe's unique form of government, its laws, its history and people. If the media truly want to cover American Indian issues, they must get to know the American Indian community and gain its trust. As I mentioned earlier, the first step is assigning a culturally sensitive reporter to a "reservation beat" so that coverage is consistent. The daily cited in the opening example might have decided upon another angle (and page) for the car accident story had it known how the deaths devastated the Indian community.

Indian media are helping to fill the gaps left by mainstream media, but we are certainly not without our shortcomings. What we do have is a commitment to providing news for American Indians—and not just about them. By portraying American Indians as people, rather than as statistics, the mainstream media would go far in dispelling persistent stereotypes of the First Americans.

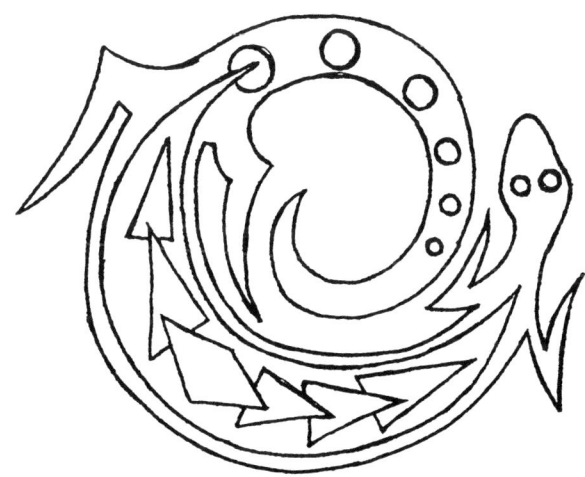

EVERY WORD OF THE ORIGINAL!

Collector's Edition

WILD WEST WEEKLY

No. 37. NEW YORK, JULY 3, 1903. Price 5 Cents.

YOUNG WILD WEST RUNNING THE GAUNTLET;
OR, THE PAWNEE CHIEF'S LAST SHOT.
By AN OLD SCOUT.

PLUS: "Dandy Dan of Deadwood" — A complete story from "Wide Awake Library"

"No white man before had survived the terrible ordeal of the Pawnee gauntlet!"

Cowboys and Indians

By Paul O. Sand

On many of those long, hot July days on the plains of west-central Minnesota, there wasn't much for a bunch of six- and seven-year-old boys to do, except to play cowboys and Indians. And there were many days when we'd gather in the woods on the edge of town with our assorted weaponry — Red Ryder BB guns, breech-loading Winchesters, six-shooters, rubber Bowie knives, and even a Daniel Boone flint gun

Before acting out our imaginative barbarianism, there would be the inevitable argument over who was going to play which role. Of course everyone, including myself, wanted to be on the winning side. That meant no one wanted to be the Indian. Everyone wanted to be either Bronco Ben, or Ugly Joe, or Blacksnake Nick, or Salamander Tom. My favorite was Dandy Dan of Deadwood, whom I played with a cunning intelligence.

The argument would last until someone would threaten to go home. That was the signal for a compromise, and more often than not, I'd end up volunteering to be the Indian. But before I did, I'd make the others promise I'd be given a "fair" chance to win. They'd solemnly agree, swear on a stack of Gideon Bibles, and even cross their hearts. Sometimes, as a token of their appreciation, they'd even let me have the youngest boy to be my comrade-in-arms.

And then — crack! whizz! thud! — the battle for the Red River Valley would begin. Yelling with vengeance, with bullets humming and crackling over my head, I'd chase Salamander Tom — a very slow and awkward lad — through bushes, and over and under fallen cottonwoods. Finally, with my knees bruised and cut, I'd corner this cowering paleface in some ditch.

It was generally at this point, when I was about to put Salamander Tom out of the business of killing Indians, that the "rules" would suddenly change. And no matter how many well-placed shots I triggered with my breech-loading Winchester, he'd somehow dodge them all, and then, with a loud whoop, charge hell-bent from the ditch. That whoop always seemed to be the signal that the rules had been changed, and that it was now "open season" on me.

After that, it was only a matter of time before they'd take me into captivity. That meant making me run through a patch of burning weeds with my pants legs rolled up. Or they'd pretend to hang me, burn me at the stake or whip me into unconsciousness. This torturing part of our play symbolized our prevailing belief that savages deserved such cruel and unusual justice.

Back then, most of our racial myths about Indians and our violent make-believe behaviour were influenced, if not conditioned, by the grade-B cowboy movies we saw free of charge on Saturday nights. There was, however, another source that nurtured our racist attitudes.

In our general store there were three old cardboard boxes filled with Buffalo Bill weekly magazines. Some of the Wild West weeklies dated as far back as 1890. Evidently, some farmer had brought the weeklies to the store, perhaps in exchange for a pair of socks or gloves, or food. They were the most popular readings among us boys.

The readings perpetuated the racial myth of the Indian as a savage and a heathen, and played an important role in forming our attitudes toward Indians.

Consider, for example, this excerpt from one of the weeklies: "Even though the government had subdued the Pawnee Indians into something like a peaceful way of living, they would break out on the warpath now and then, and return to their old habits and instincts and seek the white man's scalp."

Now, as we well know, the angel of racist

mythology is prejudice. And we also know that childhood prejudices die hard, if ever at all, a fact that was driven home to me just the other day.

Unexpectedly, one of my childhood friends — the one who always insisted on being Salamander Tom — stopped in to visit me. I hadn't seen him for more than 35 years. After getting the pleasantries — how fat and bald we had gotten — out of the way, we began recalling all the fun we had as children growing up in a small town. Then we began exchanging life experiences and telling each other what we were now doing with our lives.

At this point, things got unpleasant. For when I mentioned that I was working on a project in South Dakota, combating racial prejudice and discrimination against Native Americans, he recoiled abruptly. With triumphant ignorance and a tremor from the corner of his left eye, he proceeded to make some of the most intolerant and prejudicial remarks I've heard in a long time.

To him, Indians were naturally lazy, incorrigibly delinquent, habitually dishonest, genetically disease-ridden, and instinctively pagan. His solution to the so-called Indian problem was to abolish all reservations, eliminate all federal handouts, and throw them all into the job market. "Let them sink or swim," he said defiantly. "What they need is a heavy dose of the Protestant work ethic." And then he went on to moralize that the problems confronting Indians were a form of divine punishment for their past and present moral frailties. In short, what was happening to them was divinely deserved.

As I listened to this well-educated 50-year-old business executive, I realized that he had never outgrown the prejudices he had learned as a child. He was still Salamander Tom cowering in a ditch.

I suppose I should've explained to him that when one divides others on the basis of race or ethnic heritage, social justice is impossible. And that his kind of prejudice robs us of the many talents that Indians possess, and that the Horatio Alger myth of rugged individualism often meant getting Indians drunk to exploit them. But, rightly or wrongly, I concluded that nothing could be done for this first-class bigot of power and status. Not a lecture on the meaning of pluralistic democracy, nor an analysis of the relationship between racism and poverty would've changed his mind. Needless to say, we did not part as friends who would see each other again.

After this encounter, I began thinking about my experiences and education, and how I was able to throw off my early racist attitudes toward Indians. To be sure, this attitude was never challenged during my days in grade school, nor in high school. In fact, very little was ever mentioned in the classroom about Indian heritage. Minnesota history, which may well consist of 40 percent Indian history, was taught in the schools I attended without including the significant role of native peoples.

Nor did we have human-relations classes designed to break down racial stereotypes: that Indians were less ambitious than whites; that Indians laughed a lot; that Indians wanted to live off the federal government; and that Indians had looser morals than white people.

Only when I entered college were some of these racist stereotypes and myths challenged. In one history course — How the West Was Physically Won and Morally Lost — I read about how Indians were conquered, dispossessed, exploited, and abandoned by white people. In a sociology class, I came to understand that racism is a dogma that is religiously cultivated and transmitted and is a major factor in producing poverty.

Through anthropology courses, I learned about the Indians' concept of time as a continuum related to the rising and setting of the sun, about their attitudes toward work, about their respect for the elderly, about their need to be free and to live harmoniously with nature, and about their desire for tranquility rather than competition. What is clear about all of this is that giving human respect and dignity to those who are racially and ethnically different does not take place naturally. It must be learned through the sharing of thoughts and feelings.

It seems to me that these were the kind of cultural learning experiences Salamander

Tom never had, the experiences that he should have had. Clearly it's too late for him, but it's not too late for the generation passing through our public schools today. Racism is not inevitable; it is only so when educators and opinion-makers fail to expose students to ethical values and to challenge the cruel legacy of racism — a legacy that has made the American Indian the most victimized minority in our society.

Paul O. Sand has been the Executive Director of the National Conference on Christians and Jews, Minnesota-Dakotas Region, for seventeen years. He lectures in bio-medical ethics at the College of St. Catherine, St. Mary's Campus in Saint Paul, Minnesota, and has been a board director of the Minnesota Civil Liberties Union for ten years. He is the founder of the "Model United Nations" in the Netherlands in 1967, and has been widely published in newspapers and journals in Minnesota.

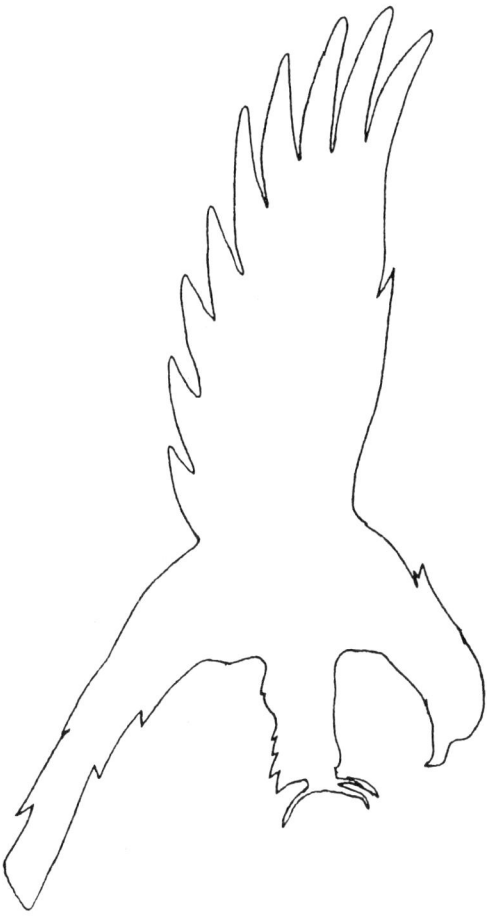

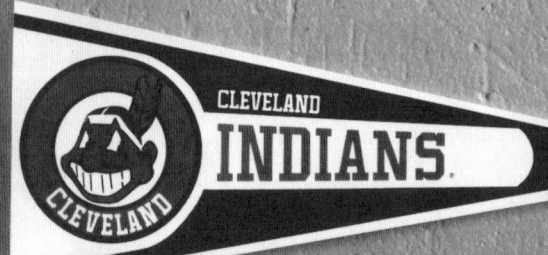

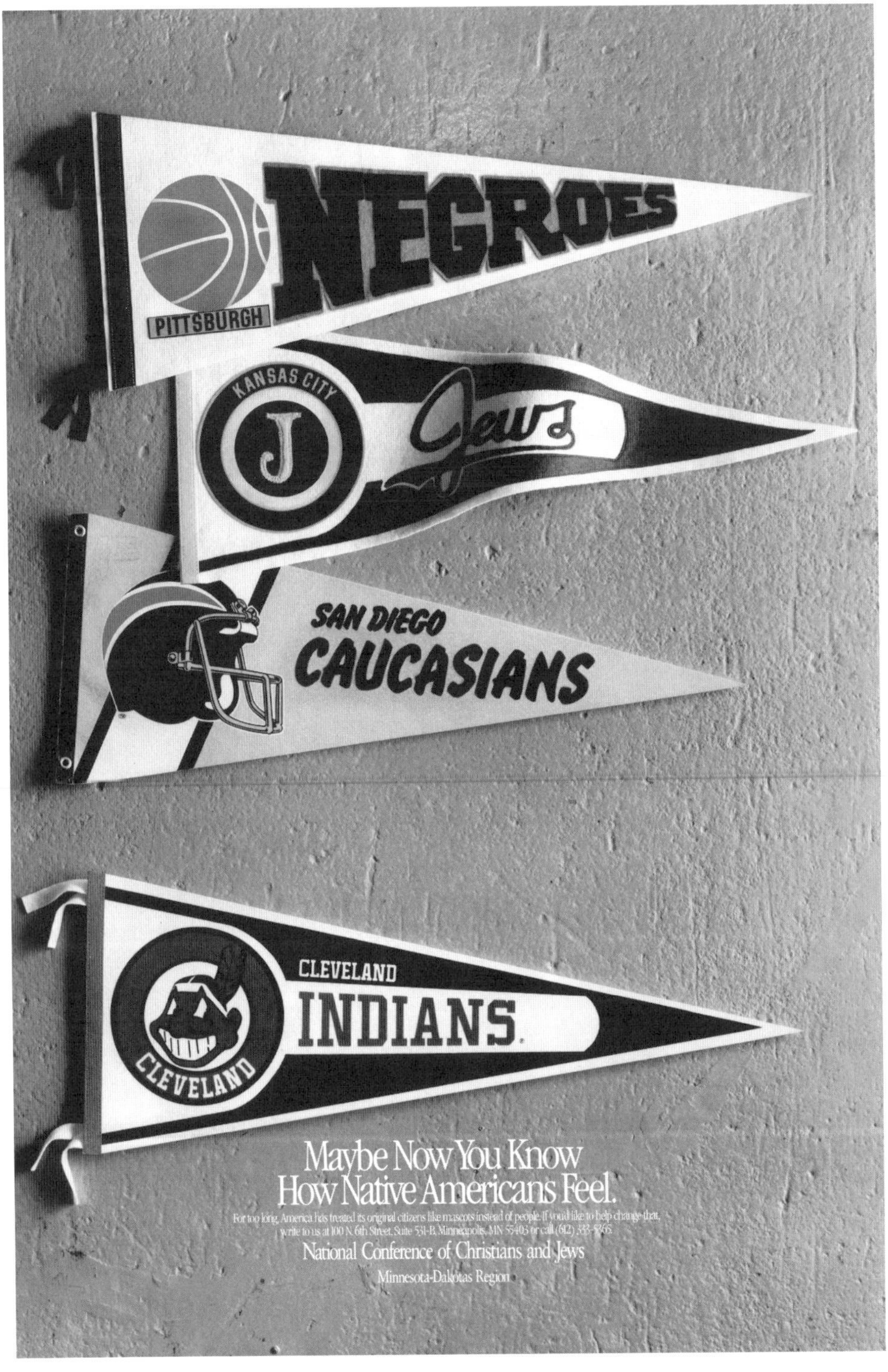
PITTSBURGH
NEGROES
KANSAS CITY
J
Jews
SAN DIEGO
CAUCASIANS
CLEVELAND
INDIANS.
CLEVELAND
Maybe Now You Know
How Native Americans Feel.
For too long, America has treated its original citizens like mascots instead of people. If you'd like to help change that, write to us at 100 N. 6th Street, Suite 531-B, Minneapolis, MN 55403 or call (612) 333-5365.
National Conference of Christians and Jews
Minnesota-Dakotas Region

Pigskin Mascots: A Seasonal Insult

By Tim Giago (Nanwica Kciji)

Autumn is in the air and so are the pigskins. As surely as the geese fly south for the winter, it's time to take my annual look at that strange, seasonal custom of Americans using a race of people as mascots for a sporting event known as football.

Now most of us have heard of the Blue Devils of Duke and the Orangemen of Syracuse, but I don't think too many Americans have ever seen a real, live blue devil or an orange man, at least not while in a state of sobriety.

As far as I can determine, there is only one species of human beings indigenous to this galaxy that have sports teams named after the color of their skin - the American Indian. We do have the Fighting Irish of Notre Dame, a team obviously named after a race of people, but they are never referred to as the "Fighting Whiteskins."

The two teams most notorious for exploiting the skin color of Native Americans are the Washington Redskins and the St. John's Redmen. Confronted by an angry assembly of Indians, a compassionate and understanding faculty changed the name of the Stanford "Indians" to the "Cardinals." The sky did not fall in on the alumni of this university because of this action.

The University of Illinois continues to have its mascot, Chief Illiniwek, cavort around the stadium and do his bad impressions of Indian dances while decked out in the attire of a Lakota (Sioux) warrior.

I have pointed out in the past that since Jack Kent Cooke, the owner of the Washington Redskins, sees nothing wrong in naming his football team after the skin color of the American Indians, he should take a look around his community and see that the predominant race residing in Washington, D. C., is black.

Mr. Cooke should consider this fact and rename his team the Washington Blackskins to honor the majority population. Because the predominant minority in San Francisco happens to be people of Asian persuasion, the San Francisco Forty Niners should take stock of this and name their team the San Francisco Yellowskins. After all, fair is fair - no pun intended - and the owners of these professional football teams should not restrict the colorlines to "Redskins."

Just think of the pageantry the Forty Niners could add to their halftime show if their team was the "Yellowskins." A mascot dressed as a Mandarin could leap about the infield while the fans in the stands could paint their faces yellow, wear long pigtails, and attempt to sing ancient Oriental songs while bashing a giant gong.

"Redskins" fans see nothing wrong in waltzing about wearing feathers, toting imitation Pipestone pipes, beating miniature drums, sporting painted faces, and conducting themselves in other bizarre ways that insult the traditions, culture and spirituality of the First Americans.

It is not so much the fact that a team is named after a race of people or the color of that people's skin, but the sham rituals and ridiculous impersonations that become a part of those rituals that are an insult to every American Indian residing on this continent.

Unless Jack Kent Cooke or the President of St. John's University has the courage to call his team Blackskins, Whiteskins, Brownskins, or Yellowskins, he does not have the right to call his team Redmen or Redskins.

The point has been made that many genuine Indian schools call themselves warriors, braves, or chiefs, but the difference here is the faculties and student bodies of these schools do not degrade the spiritual or cultural integrity of Native Americans in the process. The intent is to honor shared traditions because most of the students are

Native Americans. They are respectful and reverent in the way they represent their own people.

Suppose the Washington Redskins or the St. John's Redmen did change their names to "Blackskins". Would the fans in the stands feel comfortable painting their faces black, wearing Afro wigs and otherwise carrying out stereotypical activities that are supposedly characteristic of blacks? Not on your life . . . literally.

Then why do this to Native Americans? Remember the American Indian is a proud race. We are not mascots. We are not unfeeling objects to be held up in ridicule to an ignorant bunch of sports fans. We are human beings with dreams, with goals and ambitions. Being used as sporting mascots is not one of these goals.

Until America wakes up to this fact this nation will never know true equality, true greatness, or true democracy. It will always be a country that separates its population by the color of their skins. Is this what America truly wants?

Reprinted courtesy of the Lakota Times. *'Notes From Indian Country,' September 25, 1991.*

Tips on Covering and Portraying American Indians

By Doris J. Giago and Bill Huntzicker

Interviewing

■ Prepare yourself by doing prior research. We are a diverse people. One tribe is not the same as another; not all tribal situations are the same. Recognize differences in the groups that you cover. Understanding develops slowly and evolves from commitment.

■ Plan to check with multiple sources. One Indian cannot speak for all Indians.

■ Dress appropriately—dress can put up barriers between people. A three-piece suit is too extreme, it will stop people. But don't go to the other extreme and dress too sloppily. Casual dress is usually appropriate.

■ On a first visit it may be a good idea to drive around the reservation to get accustomed to the place before you interview.

■ Look for positive stories.

■ Talk directly with the people involved.

■ Deal with people instead of types.

■ Don't be aggressive. Don't come to the Indian people with lots of rules.

■ Try to understand and be sensitive about cultural differences. Things appropriate to non-Indians may not be appropriate to Indians. Cultural assistance from a member of a group is like a gift. Be open to alternative ways of looking at the world.

■ A non-Indian interviewing on the reservation may take some getting acquainted with living conditions. A reservation home may take getting used to. Don't make judgements about living conditions.

■ The ideal situation for an interview is one-on-one . . . it's more personal. But be prepared to adjust to conditions.

■ Take the time to make your interviewee comfortable. Keep in mind that Indian people have a great sense of humor, and keep

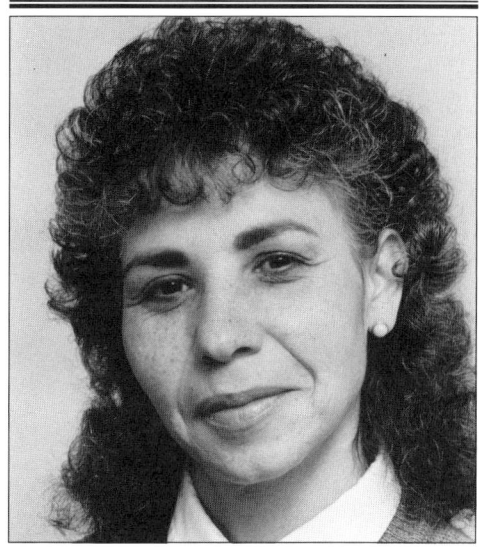

DORIS GIAGO
Doris J. Giago is Oglala Sioux and holds a degree from South Dakota State University. She is one of the founders of the *Lakota Times.* She is presently completing a Masters Degree in Journalism and will be teaching at South Dakota State University in the Fall semester of 1992.

the humor appropriate. Stay away from stereotypes. Be flexible with regard to "Indian time". A no-nonsense, clock-bound pace may not be appropriate. Let things flow rather than worrying about the clock.

■ Don't be concerned with lack of eye contact. This is a cultural matter.

■ Be flexible about Indian ways. For example, praying with the medicine man before you interview him.

■ Be prepared for pauses and silences. With the elderly, especially, don't assume that because they have their eyes closed they are not listening or have fallen asleep. This is a way to avoid outside interference in order to concentrate on the issue.

■ Be willing to go with the directions that the interviewee takes. Don't get stuck on a fixed set of questions. Be a good listener. As journalists we may expect to get certain responses to our questions. But our expectations may not be accurate.

Reporting

■ Be aware of stereotypes so that you can avoid them. Present the evidence rather than disputing the stereotypes.

■ Avoid blaming the victim; avoid assumptions.

■ A lot of problems with non-Indian coverage of Indian people are related to attempts to be conclusive. Let the report be open-ended.

■ Coverage should be suggestive rather than declarative.

■ Coverage should be a composite rather than a summary—a mosaic rather than an equation.

■ Don't cast aspersions.

■ Assume treaty rights are correct and are basic rights.

■ Assume that the present has risen out of the past; there is a continuity.

■ Assume that land rights are real.

■ Don't look for good guys and bad guys.

■ Check back with your sources regarding important parts of the piece, so that you produce a true, fair piece of work.

■ Question the inevitability of progress.

Bill Huntzicker is a lecturer in the School of Journalism and Mass Communication at the University of Minnesota. His articles on images of the West in 19th century media have appeared in academic journals. Originally from Miles City, Montana he holds a bachelor of arts degree in history from Montana State University and a Ph.D. in American Studies from the University of Minnesota.

Attack on Sovereignty Relentless

By Roger Jourdain

The sovereign rights of the American Indian Nations are under attack. I know this is not anything new to you people gathered here today but I believe the attacks are growing more and more vocal.

All we need to do is to look at the news reports of the lunatics who are trying to organize nationally to "modernize" our treaties.

Modernize, that's their new buzz word for abrogation.

The sovereignty of tribal nations has been under attack since 1492. For 500 years the tribal nations have been fighting to protect their people, their lands and their resources from the greed of the white man.

The first policy of the white man was that of genocide. The fact that there are some of us here today demonstrates the failure of that policy. However, they did manage to exterminate 80 percent of our people by the end of the 19th century.

In comparison, Hitler managed to eradicate only 50 percent of the Jews in World War II. While that policy has been universally condemned by world opinion, few of the national or international leaders have expressed similar concern for American Indians.

The attack on tribal sovereignty is taking many forms — from protests of our aboriginal hunting and fishing rights to the enactment of national legislation that takes away our right to regulate our own gaming enterprises with the National Indian Gaming Act.

(Editor's Note***This is the text of an address given at St. Cloud State University, Minnesota, May 3, 1990. It embodies the message of tribal sovereignty delivered to Indian people across America, over and over, by Roger Jourdain, former chairman of the Red Lake Band of Chippewa.)

When that legislation was first proposed back in 1982 I warned those who were involved that they would be falling into federal entrapment. They didn't listen. They went right along and helped the federal government in formulating a law that will force tribes to pay 5 percent of their gross earnings to support a national gaming commission.

In addition, it will impose a federal income tax on any per-capita payments made to tribal members from gaming profits. Tribal nations are also required to sign compacts with states so they can operate certain games.

I believe any tribal nation who joins with a state in order to comply with that stupid legislation is simply giving away a part of their sovereignty.

Wendell Chino, Art Gahbow, and I refuse to recognize a law that takes away our tribal sovereignty. We filed a lawsuit against the U.S. Government and requested other tribes to join with us.

The Red Lake Band of Chippewa will never agree to voluntarily give up our sovereignty and permit federal or state intrusion into our affairs.

The Red Lake Chippewa are moving more and more in the direction of running our own affairs without the meddlesome bureaucracy of the federal government.

On July 6, 1989, we signed a historic agreement with the U.S. Government in which we assumed executive direction of the Red Lake Bureau of Indian Affairs Agency.

We are now in the process of assuming the direction and control of the Red Lake health services. Included in that system is the Red Lake Hospital, an extended health care facility and the comprehensive health care services of the entire reservation. We are going to demonstrate that we can provide better services than either the BIA or the Indian Health Service.

The only thing we have to fear is the concentrated attacks on our tribal sovereignty. As I have said, those attacks take many forms. One of the most persistent forms is that posed by legislation or the subversion of the law.

When the Europeans first came to our country there was a common understanding that the land could not be taken except by purchase or negotiation. After the United States was formed, that concept was subverted by the Supreme Court.

First the Supreme Court refused to recognize Indian Nations as holding title to their land. Then in a series of cases, the Supreme Court began to rely on the "Doctrine of Discovery" which purportedly gave the United States superior title to all Indian Lands.

In a major subversion of the law in 1954, the Tee-Hit-Ton case, the Supreme Court decided that Indians are not entitled to be paid for their lands unless their tribal ownership has been recognized by congressional statute or by treaty.

But even tribes with treaty or executive-order reservations are not safe. The General Allotment Act of 1887 furthered the doctrine of genocide in that it sought to destroy the tribal land base and for many tribes it nearly did so.

The Red Lake Band of Chippewa were able to avoid this fate only through the strong and united stand of the traditional chiefs who refused to accept the conditions of allotment. We still hold all of our land in common ownership. For most tribes that destruction ended with the Indian Reorganization Act of 1934.

Even so, the attack on tribal sovereignty continues. In 1989, in the *Brendal* opinion, the Supreme Court said that whenever a piece of land inside a reservation goes out of trust, a little bit of tribal sovereignty goes with it. According to our tribal attorney, the *Brendal* opinion will be used by every federal court from federal district courts to the Supreme Court to destroy tribal sovereignty in the future.

What is the response of tribal leaders?

Our response in the past has been to rely on the BIA which I have characterized as the first instance of organized crime on Indian reservations.

Our response has been to rely on the National Congress of American Indians, an organization which has been ineffective over the past few years and has spent most of its time furthering its own objectives.

Our response has been to allow the National Tribal Chairmen's Association to die for lack of funding.

Our response has been to fight each other for 131A and other federal funding while tribal sovereignty has been hacked up and destroyed by the enemies of tribal government. Tribal leaders must get together and fight for our sovereignty.

Chino and I have been fighting for this all our lives. Have we forgotten the lessons of our history?

Are we unwilling to plan for the future and take the necessary steps to protect our tribal sovereignty? If so, it may be that the policy of genocide has succeeded more than we know.

In 1986, Chino and I called together a group of elected tribal leaders in Kansas City. Our purpose was to start a process where we would take all the necessary steps to ensure the sovereign status of Indian nations into perpetuity.

We were able to persuade the Senate to adopt Senate Concurrent Resolution 76 which did three things:

1. It reaffirmed the constitutionally recognized government-to-government relationship with the Indian nations which has historically been the cornerstone of this nation's official Indian policy.

2. It reaffirmed the trust responsibility of the federal government to the Indian nations.

3. It acknowledged the need for the utmost good faith in upholding the treaties as the legal and moral duty of a great nation.

On September 17, 1987, the 200th anniversary of the signing of the U.S. Constitution, (Senator Daniel Inouye, Democrat-Hawaii), participated in a traditional pipe ceremony conducted by the Red Lake Chippewa in honor of Senate Concurrent Resolution 76.

Then on October 4, 1988, the U.S. House of Representatives adopted House Concurrent Resolution 331 to the exact same effect as Resolution 76.

Another threatening piece of federal legislation that has been around since the Eisenhower Administration is House Concurrent Resolution 108, the Termination Bill. One of our objectives was to work to get that bill repudiated once and for all. It was repealed by Public Law 100-297 in 1988.

Now more action is needed. We need to make the same kind of commitment to action that all those anti-Indian organizations have made. The 131A, the federal and state governments, the anti-Indian people, they never stop trying to undermine us, our tribes, our sovereignty and everything we stand for.

The Alliance was formed in 1986 by tribes who believe we can no longer sit by and watch our national organizations do nothing.

We propose that Indian nations take over the functions of 131A agencies on their reservations and that funds being needlessly wasted in area offices be channeled into tribal programs.

We propose that Indian tribes join the Alliance in becoming an effective force in Congress.

We propose to stop the further destruction of tribal sovereignty and we ask every Indian tribal government to join us in that effort. We ask those of you here today to join us in that effort.

Reprinted courtesy of the Lakota Times, *Native American Publishing. Volume 10 Issue 50, June 12, 1991.*

"...we really don't trust the media."

By Paul O. Sand

Recently an American Indian from South Dakota told me: "We'd rather be ignored completely by the media than continue reading and hearing about only the horrific things Indians do. That kind of coverage doesn't help our self-image any. It's very painful especially to those of us who lack self-esteem and self-confidence. You know, we really don't trust the media."

In answering such a charge, the media generally point out that since the public has a constitutional right-to-know what is happening, the reporter's only professional duty is to tell it all. That duty in the eyes and ears of most media professionals outweighs any concern that such reporting could reinforce negative images of Indians in the minds of racists.

Most of all, what it tells us about the current nature of the moral and ethical problem between American Indians and the mass media is that many editors, reporters, commentators, broadcasters, directors and producers treat Indians as object-bodies, or as passive psychological "Its."

The chief sins of commission and omission concerning the lack of human compassion in reporting seem to point to the technical training that mass communicators receive in schools. There is too much emphasis placed on developing skills in writing with detached brevity and speaking with affective neutrality. It also appears that too much time is spent on being clear, concise, coherent and correct in reporting, as well as being markedly proficient in the mechanics of the who, what, when, where, why and how of writing news stories.

As things seem to stand, mass communicators spend too little time developing the skills of consideration for others and of sensitivity to the potential harm their reporting may cause. To be considerate is to be aware of the fears and anxieties of their subjects and readers. To be considerate is to practice the media ethic "do unto others as you would have them do unto you."

Without question, our schools of journalism turn out very talented technicians. But they are technicians who, more often than not, lack compassionate care in reporting on people who live outside the "white" mainstream of our society. The little media coverage given to Indian affairs ignores the importance Indians place on their sovereignty and treaties, and on the philosophical and historical dynamics of their cultures. There is also evidence that coverage of Indian issues lacks balanced reporting. The negative aspects are over-exposed, while positive events are under-reported.

To put the matter more bluntly, the media should begin educating themselves, especially editors and upper media executives, to the reasons why so many Indians have such a low sense of self-worth and why their reporting carries the potential for inflicting great psychological suffering on Indian people, or for that matter, any other minority group.

The key question, as I see it, is; how can the mass media present to the public the plight of Native Americans?

Perhaps one way would be to have a major television network produce a miniseries of the past and present genocidal, racist and dehumanizing treatment of American Indians. Such a production should be on the same scale as Roots and the Holocaust. What has been done for Blacks and for Jews, by exposing to the general public the roots of prejudice and hatred which caused them unmeasurable pain, suffering and death, can most certainly be done for Indians.

No Indian history course in high school or in college could have more of a moral and ethical impact on non-Indians than a production documenting the brutal and deathly journey of Indians across their own heartland. Such a production could create not only a positive image of Indians, but could also help them in regaining their self-identity, self-dignity and self-worth.

If whites who see themselves as the dominant race refuse to learn about and respect Indian culture and values, if social institutions, like the mass media, are unwilling to see Indians as persons, and if social equality continues to be blocked by the racist attitudes of those in power positions, then the tragic plight of American Indians will continue, until the time they are no more.

POSITIVE IMAGES

There are many American Indian heroes across the country, role models celebrated in their communities. Whether elders or peers, they are working to improve the quality of life, and the media is a tool to highlight their efforts.

This sampling does not speak for all Indian people. There is a wealth of individuals who positively influence the lives of Indians and non-Indians alike. Print and broadcast media professionals are encouraged to profile and access American Indian community leaders and role models, positive images for today's readers and viewers.

TOM BEAVER

TOM BEAVER is a former reporter, producer, Midday News anchor, and public service director with WCCO-Television in Minneapolis. Presently, he is the Director of Public Information for the Office of the Associate Provost and Associate Vice President for Academic Affairs at the University of Minnesota.

CARTER BLUE CLARK

CARTER BLUE CLARK is the Executive Vice President of Oklahoma City University. He is a member of the Muscogee (Creek) Nation. Clark has a long list of publications dealing with his interests in the historiography of the Indians of the Americas.

WENDELL CHINO

WENDELL CHINO is the chairman, president and chief executive officer of the Mescalero Apache Nation, a position he has held since 1953. He successfully pressed for changes in public housing laws in 1955 that, for the first time, allowed federal housing funds to be used on Indian reservations. Mr. Chino has effectively implemented a comprehensive plan, stressing economic and social development, as well as improvement in the health care system and political modernization. His top priority today is to establish a secure legal foundation for the tribe's sovereignty and to ensure the survival of the Mescalero Apache Nation.

STEVE CROW is a Cherokee original from Alabama. He is a pilot, poet and college professor. His poetry has appeared in more than thirty anthologies and magazines.

STEVE CROW

VINE DELORIA, JR.

VINE DELORIA, JR. is a lawyer and political science professor. He is a member of the Standing Rock Sioux Nation, Yankton, SD. His first book *Custer Died for Your Sins* brought him national attention and won several awards. Custer has been followed by a number of other books (see Bibliography).

TIM GIAGO is the author of *Aboriginal Sin* and *Notes From Indian Country,* he is from the Pine Ridge Indian Reservation in South Dakota. He is the editor of the *Lakota Times* and recipient of the 1985 H. L. Mencken Award.

TIM GIAGO

WALTER ECHO-HAWK

WALTER ECHO-HAWK is the senior staff attorney of the Native American Rights Fund (NARF). He has been active in the issue of the desecration of Indian graves, work that has been profiled in *People* magazine. Echo-Hawk is a member of the Pawnee Nation of Oklahoma.

LADONNA HARRIS is a leader in the fight for social welfare and minority rights. She is Comanche from Oklahoma. The wife of former United States Senator Fred Harris, she has been instrumental in organizing Americans for Indian Opportunity and Oklahomans for Indian Opportunity.

LADONNA HARRIS

OSCAR HOWE

OSCAR HOWE was from the Crow Creek Reservation, and a member of the Yakantonai Sioux Nation. Howe worked to objectify the truths of Indian culture. He has been characterized as a cubist, a natural evolution from the Sioux "straight line," an artistic form which symbolizes truth or righteousness.

ROGER JOURDAIN became accessible to the Indian public as a postmaster in the fifties and began to act as their advocate. He worked with the Head Hereditary Chief, August King, to set up the first secret ballot on a reservation and in 1959 was elected the first Chairman of the Red Lake Band of Chippewa and served for three decades. He celebrated his seventy-ninth birthday in July of 1991, having dedicated more than half of his life to serving and honoring American Indian people. He has looked beyond the scope of tribal politics to examine the ramifications of decisions which have affected all Indian nations. Mr. Jourdain has become famous as a national spokesman in American Indian affairs, especially for protecting tribal sovereignty and the government-to-government political relationship which exists between the federal government and Indian tribes. His contributions to health, housing, economic development and other issues have also had significant impact on tribes across the country.

ROGER JOURDAIN

GERALDINE KEAMS

GERALDINE KEAMS is from the Navajo Nation in the Painted Desert region of Arizona. She is an actress, storyteller, poet, and writer. She is the President of Hozhoni Films, and an independent producer. She dedicates time and creative energy to keeping the oral tradition of American Indian legends alive.

WILMA P. MANKILLER

WILMA P. MANKILLER is the Principal Chief of the Cherokee Nation. She is the first woman to hold this position and it has brought national and international media attention to the Cherokee Nation. Chief Mankiller's philosophy is based on empowering the people at the local level. She strongly encourages the tribal membership to become more self-reliant. In addition to her interest in community development, she devotes her time and expertise in intergovernmental relations to bring about an enlightened State and Congressional response to American Indian concerns.

N. SCOTT MOMADAY

N. SCOTT MOMADAY is a member of the Eastern Cherokee Nation and Pulitzer Prize winning novelist. He has published several volumes of poetry. Momaday has completed a documentary series, *More Than Bows and Arrows,* that acknowledges the contributions of American Indians.

KELLY MOORE, a member of the Creek Nation, is a doctor of medicine and is married with two children, Matthew and Tava. She is the Clinical Director and medical staff supervisor at the Hu Hu Kam ("those who have gone" in Pima) Memorial Hospital in Sacaton, Arizona on the Gila River Reservation. Dr. Moore is an officer with the Public Health Service Commissioned Corps, a fellow of the American Academy of Pediatrics, and a member of the Association of American Indian Physicians.

KELLY MOORE

CORNEL PEWEWARDY

CORNEL PEWEWARDY is the principal of the recently established American Indian Magnet School in St. Paul, MN. Dr. Pewewardy is not only a noted academic, but has served on tribal advisory councils, and state textbook review committees. He is a member of the Comanche-Kiowa Nation of Oklahoma.

MARIA TALLCHIEF

MARIA TALLCHIEF was a member of the Osage Nation. She was a prominent Ballerina and danced with the Ballet Russe de Monte Carlo and the New York City Ballet. From 1947 to 1960 she was Prima Ballerina for the company. She founded the Chicago City Ballet in 1980.

THE TURTLE MOUNTAIN BOYS

THE TURTLE MOUNTAIN BOYS, Turtle Mountain Chippewa from North Dakota, from left to right — J.J. (Thomas) Gourneau, Wayne Poitra, Sr., Alan Page, Les Thomas, and Kevin Keplin. Although the all-Indian country rock band are well respected in the music industry their interest is not only in their own music but also in getting exposure for Turtle Mountain artistic talent. Les Thomas, the chairman for the tribally-funded artist board which also promotes sculpture, painting, basketry, and bead work, "wants to promote a positive image of the reservation."

GAE VEIT

GAE VEIT is the founder/owner of Shingobee Builders, construction company. She was honored as the "Entrepreneur of the Year" in Washington, D.C. by President Bush in October 1991. In August, 1986 Gae Veit helped to form the Minnesota American Indian Chamber of Commerce which includes American Indian business owners and professionals in a wide variety of businesses and professions.

JOANNE WHITERABBIT is Manager of Volunteer/Community Relations for Cray Research, Inc. and Manager of Diversity Programs for the Cray Research Foundation, in Minneapolis. She is working with other employees to implement the Global Action Plan for Earth.

JOANNE WHITERABBIT

RESOURCE DIRECTORY

The criteria for covering Indian stories is the same as any other, although the quest for impartiality and sensitivity may require looking beyond traditional sources. Dig a little deeper, accessing new contacts both inside and outside Indian communities. This directory is a place to begin.

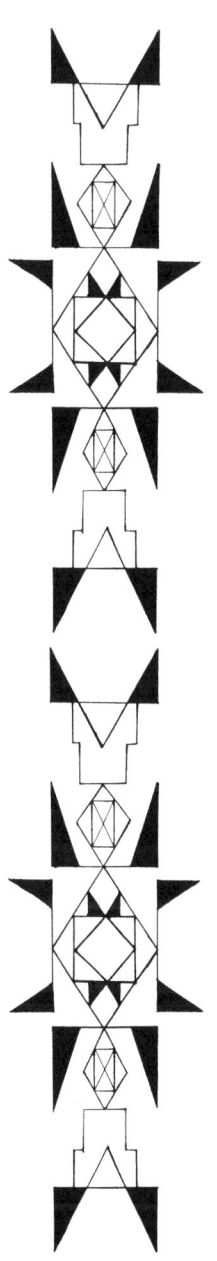

NATIONAL COUNCILS

National councils create tribal policy and govern tribal and reservation affairs.

ALABAMA
Poarch Band of Creek Indians
Rte. 3, P. O. Box 243-A
Atmore, AL 36502
(205) 368-9136
Nation: Creek

ALASKA
Arctic Village Traditional
Council
P. O. Box 22050
Arctic Village, AK 99722
(907) 587-5226
Nation: Gwitch'in Athapascan

Bering Straits Native
Corporation
P. O. Box 1008
Nome, AK 99762
(907) 443-5252

Bristol Bay Native Association
P. O. Box 179
Dillingham, AK 99576
(907) 842-5257

Calista Corporation
601 W 5th #200
Anchorage, AK 99501
(907) 279-5516

Chugach Natives, Inc.
Anchorage, AK 99503
(907)276-1080

Cook Inlet Native Association
Anchorage, AK 99503
(907) 278-4641

Copper River Native
Association
P.O. Drawer H
Copper River, AK 99673
(907) 822-5241

Kawerak, Incorporated
P. O. Box 505
Nome, AK 99762
(907) 443-5231

Kenaitze Indian Tribal Council
P. O. Box 988
Kenai, AK 99611
(907) 283-3633

Kodiak Area Native Association
402 Center Ave.
Kodiak, AK 99615
(907) 486-5725

Koniag, Incorporated
P. O. Box 746
Kodiak, AK 99615
(907) 486-4147

Manilaq Incorporated
P. O. Box 257
Kotzebue, AK 99752
(907) 442-3311

Nana Regional Corporation
P. O. Box 49
Kotzebue, AK 99752
(907) 442-3301

North Pacific Rim Native
Association
Anchorage, AK 99503
(907) 276-2121

Sealaska Corporation
One Sealaska Plaza, Suite 400
Juneau, AK 99801
(907) 586-1512

Tanana Chiefs Conference
122 1st Ave.
Fairbanks, AK 99701
(907) 456-1275

Tlingit/Haida Central Council
320 W Willoughby Ave.,
Suite 300
Juneau, AK 99801
(907) 585-1432
Nation: Tlingit and Haida

ARIZONA
AK Chin Indian
Community Council
Rte . 2, P. O. Box 27
Maricopa, AZ 85239
(602) 568-2227
Nation: Papago

Cocopah Tribal Council
P. O. Box Bin G
Somerton, AZ 85350
(602) 627-2102
Nation: Cocopah

Colorado River Indian Tribal
Council
Rte. 1, P. O. Box 23-B
Parker, AZ 85344
(602) 669-9211
Nation: Mohave, Chemehuevi,
Hopi and Navajo

Gila River Indian
Community Council
P. O. Box 97
Sacaton, AZ 85247
(602) 562-3311
Nation: Pima and Maricopa

Havasupai Tribal Council
P. O. Box 10
Supai, AZ 86435
(602) 448-2961
Nation: Havasupai

NATIONAL COUNCILS

Hopi Tribal Council
P. O. Box 123
Kykotsmovi, AZ 86039
(602) 734-2445
Nation: Hopi and Tewa

Hualapai Tribal Council
P. O. Box 168
Peach Springs, AZ 86434
(602) 769-2216
Nation: Hualapai

Kaibab Paiute Tribal Council
Tribal Affairs Bldg.
Pipe Springs, AZ 86022
(602) 643-7245
Nation: Paiute

Mohave-Apache Community Council
P. O. Box 17779
Fountain Hills, AZ 85268
(602) 990-0995
Nation: Mohave and Apache

Navajo Tribal Council
P. O. Box 308
Window Rock, AZ 86515
(602) 871-4941
Nation: Navajo

Pascua Yaqui Tribal Council
7474 S. Camino De Oeste
Tuscon, AZ 85746
(602) 883-2838
Nation: Pascua Yaqui

Quechan Tribal Council
P. O. Box 1352
Yuma, AZ 85364
(602) 572-0213
Nation: Quechan

Salt River Pima-Maricopa Indian Community Council
Rte. 1, P. O. Box 216
Scottsdale, AZ 85256
(602) 941-72777
Nation: Pima and Maricopa

San Carlos Tribal Council
P. O. Box 0
San Carlos, AZ 85550
(602) 475-2361
Nation; San Carlos Apache

Tohono O'Odham Council
P. O. Box 837
Sells, AZ 85634
(602) 383-2221
Nation: Papago

Tonto Apache Tribal Council
Tonto Reservation #30
Payson, AZ 85541
(602) 474-5000

White Mountain Apache Tribal Council
P. O. Box 700
Whiteriver, AZ 85941
(602) 338-4346
Nation: Apache

Yavapai-Apache Community Council
P. O. Box 1188
Camp Verde, AZ 86322
(602) 567-3649
Nation: Yavapai-Apache

CALIFORNIA

Agua Caliente Tribal Council
960 E. Tahquitz Way #106
Palm Springs, CA 92262
(619) 325-5673
Nation: Cahuilla

Barona General Business Council
1095 Barona Rd.
Lakeside, CA 92040
(619) 433-6612
Nation: Diegueno

Berry Creek Rancheria Tribal Council
1779 Mitchell Ave.
Oroville, CA 95966
(916) 534-3895
Nation: Tyme Maidu

Big Bend General Council
P. O. Box 255
Big, Bend, CA 96001
(916) 337-6605
Nation: Pit River

Big Lagoon Council
P. O. Box 3060
Trinidad, CA 95570
(707) 826-2079
Nation: Yurok and Tolowa

Big Pine General Council
P. O. Box 700
Big Pine, CA 93513
(619) 938-2121
Nation: Paiute and Shoshone

Bishop Indian Tribal Council
P. O. Box 548
Bishop, CA 93514
(619) 873-3584
Nation: Paiute and Shoshone

Blue Lake Rancheria Council
P. O. Box 428
Blue Lake, CA 95525
(707) 668-5005

Bridgeport General Council
P. O. Box 37
Bridgeport, CA 93517
(619) 932-7083
Nation: Paiute

Cabazon General Council
84-245 Indio Spring Dr.
Indio, CA 92201
(619) 342-2593
Nation: Cahuilla

Cahuilla General Council
1779 Campo Truck Trail
Campo, CA 92006
(619) 478-9046
Nation: Diegueno

Cedarville Community Council
P. O. Box 142
Cedarville, CA 96104
Nation: Paiute

Chemehuevi Tribal Council
P. O. Box 1976
Chemehuevi Valley, CA 92363
(619) 858-4531
Nation: Chemehuevi

Chicken Ranch Rancheria Council
P. O. Box 1699
Jamestown, CA 95327
(209) 984-3057

Cold Springs Tribal Council
P. O. Box 209
Tollhouse, CA 93667
(209) 855-2326
Nation: Mono

NATIONAL COUNCILS

Colusa Indian Community
Council
P. O. Box 8
Colusa, CA 95932
(916) 458-8231
Nation: Wintun

Covelo Community Council
Round Valley Reservation
P. O. Box 448
Covelo, CA 95428
(707) 983-6126
Nation: Maidu

Coyote Valley Interim
Tribal Council
P. O. Box 39
Redwood Valley, CA 95470
(707) 485-8723
Nation: Pomo

Cuyapaipe General Council
P. O. Box 471
Alpine, CA 92001
(619) 478-5289
Nation: Diegueno

Dry Creek Tribal Council
P. O. Box 607
Geyserville, CA 95441
(707) 433-8232
Nation: Pomo

Elem General Council
Sulphur Bank Rancheria
P. O. Box 618
Clearlake Oaks, CA 95423
(707) 998-3315
Nation: Pomo

Enterprise Rancheria
7470 Feather Falls Star Route
Oroville, CA 95965
(916) 589-0652
Nation: Maidu

Fort Bidwell Community
Council
P. O. Box 127
Fort Bidwell, CA 96112
(916) 279-6310
Nation: Paiute

Fort Independence General
Council
P. O. Box 67
Independence, CA 93526
(619) 878-2126
Nation: Paiute

Fort Mojave Tribal Council
500 Merriman Ave.
Needles, CA 92363
(619) 326-4591
Nation: Mojave

Greenville General Council
P. O. Box 237
Greenville, CA 95947
(916) 284-6446

Grindstone General Council
P. O. Box 63
Elk Creek, CA 95939
(916) 968-5116
Nation: Wintun

Hoopa Valley Business Council
P. O. Box 1348
Hoopa, CA 95546
(916) 625-4211
Nation: Hoopa

Hopland Interim Tribal Council
P. O. Box 610
Hopland, CA 95449
(707) 744-1647

Inaja & Cosmit General Council
739 A St., Apt. 12
Ramona, CA 92065
(619) 789-8581
Nation: Diegueno

Jackson Interim Council
1600 Bingo Way
Jackson, CA 95642
(209) 223-3931
Nation: Miwok

Jamul General Council
P. O. Box 612
Jamul, CA 92035
(619) 697-5041

Kashia Business Committee
Stewarts Point Rancheria
P. O. Box 54
Stewarts Point, CA 95480
(707) 785-2594
Nation: Kashia-Pomo

La Jolle General Council
Star Route, P. O. Box 158
Valley Center, CA 92082
(619) 742-3771
Nation: Luiseno

La Posta General Council
P. O. Box 894
Boulevard, CA 92005
(619) 478-5523
Nation: Luiseno

Laytonville General Council
P. O. Box 1239
Laytonville, CA 95454
(707) 984-6197
Nation: Cahto-Pomo

Lone Pine Tribal Council
Star Route
1101 South Main St.
Lone Pine, CA 93545
(619) 876-5414
Nation: Paiute-Shoshone

Lookout Rancheria Council
P. O. Box 87
Lookout, CA 96054
Nation: Pit River

Los Coyotes General Council
P. O. Box 249
Warner Springs, CA 92086
(619) 782-3269
Nation: Luiseno

Manchester/Port Arena
Community Council
P. O. Box 623
Point Arena, CA 95468
(707) 882-2788
Nation: Pomo

Manzanita General Council
P. O. Box 1302
Boulevard, CA 92005
(619) 478-5028
Nation: Diequeno

Mesa Grande General Council
P. O. Box 270
Santa Ysabel, CA 92070
(619) 782-3835
Nation: Diegueno

Middletown Interim Council
P. O. Box 292
Middletown, CA 95461
Nation: Pomo

Mooretown Rancheria Council
1900 Oro Dam Blvd. #8
Oroville, CA 95965
(916) 533-3625

40

NATIONAL COUNCILS

Morongo General Council
11581 Potrero Rd.
Banning, CA 92220
(714) 849-4697
Nation: Serrano

Pala General Council
P. O. Box 43
Pala, CA 92059
(619) 742-3784
Nation: Cupa

Pauma General Council
P. O. Box 86
Pauma Valley, CA 92061
(619) 742-1289
Nation: Luiseno

Pechanga Tribal Council
P. O. Box 1477
Temecula, CA 92390
(714) 676-2768
Nation: Luiseno

Picayune Rancherria
P. O. Box 708
Coorsegold, CA 93614
(209) 683-6633

Pinoleville Rancheria
367 N State St., Suite 204
Ukiah, CA
(707) 463-1454

Pit River Tribal Council
P.O. Drawer 1570
Burney, CA 96013
(916) 335-5421
Nation: Pit River

Potter Valley Rancheria
P. O. Box 94
Potter Valley, CA 95469
(707) 743-1649

Redding Rancheria
1786 California St.
Redding, CA 96001
(916) 241-1871

Redwood Valley Rancheria
P. O. Box 499
Redwood Valley, CA 95470
(707) 485-0361

Resighini Business Council
P. O. Box 529
Klamath, CA 95548
(707) 482-2431
Nation: Yurok

Rincon Business Committee
P. O. Box 68
Valley Center, CA 92082
(619) 749-1051
Nation: Luiseno

Robinson Citizens Business Council
P. O. Box 1119
Nice, CA 95464
(707) 275-0527
Nation: Pomo

Rohnerville Rancheria
P. O. Box 108
Eureka, CA 95501
(707) 442-3931

Round Valley General Council
P. O. Box 448
Covelo, CA 95428
(707) 983-6126

Rumsey Community Council
P. O. Box 18
Brooks, CA 95606
(916) 796-3400
Nation: Wintun

San Mauel General Council
5438 North Victoria Ave.
Highland, CA 92346
(714) 864-3686
Nation: Serrano

San Pasqual General Council
P. O. Box 365
Valley Center, CA 92082
(619) 749-3200
Nation: Luiseno

Santa Rose General Council
16835 Alkali Dr.
Lemoore, CA 93245
(209) 924-1278
Nation: Cahuilla

Santa Ynez General Council
P. O. Box 517
Santa Ynez, CA 93460
(805) 688-7997
Nation: Chumash

Santa Ysabel General Council
P. O. Box 126
Santa Ysabel, CA 92070
(619) 765-0845
Nation: Diegueno

Sherwood Valley General Council
2141 South State St.
Ukiah, CA 95482
(707) 468-1337
Nation: Pomo

Shingle Springs Rancheria
P. O. Box 1340
Shingle Springs, CA 95682
(619) 676-8010
Nation: Miwok

Smith River Rancheria
P. O. Box 239
Smith River, CA 95567
(707) 487-9255

Soboba General Council
P. O. Box 487
San Jacinto, CA 92383
(714) 654-2765
Nation: Luiseno

Susanville Indian Rancheria
Business Council
Drawer U
Susanville, CA 96130
(916) 257-6264
Nation: Paiute, Maidu and Pit River

Sycuan Business Committee
5441 Dehesa Rd.
El Cajon, CA 92021
(619) 445-5993
Nation: Diegueno

Table Bluff Board of Directors
P. O. Box 519
Loleta, CA 95551
(707) 733-5055
Nation: Wiyot

Table Mountain Interim Tribal Council
P. O. Box 243
Friant, CA 93626
(209) 822-2125

Torres-Martinez Business Council
66-725 Martinez Rd.
Thermal, CA 92274
(619) 387-0300
Nation: Cahuilla

NATIONAL COUNCILS

Trinidad Community Council
P. O. Box 630
Trinidad, CA 95570
(707) 677-0211
Nation: Yurok

Tule River Tribal Council
P. O. Box 589
Porterville, CA 93258
(209) 781-4271
Nation: Tule River

Tuolomne Me-Wuk Community Council
P. O. Box 699
Tuolumnne, CA 95379
(209) 928-4277
Nation: Miwok

Upper Lake Pomo
Tribal Council
Upper Lake Rancheria
P. O. Box 20272
Sacramento, CA 95820
(916) 371-2576

Utu Utu Gwanitu Paiute Tribal Council
Benton Paiute Reservation
Star Route 4, P. O. Box 56-A
Benton, CA 93512
(619) 933-2321
Nation: Paiute

Viejas Tribal Council
P. O. Box 908
Alpine, CA 92001
(619) 445-3810
Nation: Diegueno

Woodfords Community Council
Rte. 1, P. O. Box 102
Markleeville, CA 96120
(916) 694-2170
Nation: Washoe

COLORADO

Southern Ute Tribal Council
P. O. Box 737
Ignacio, CO 81137
(303) 563-4525
Nation: Southern Ute

Ute Mountain Ute
Tribal Council
Tribal Office Bldg.
Towaoc, CO 81344
(303) 565-3751
Nation: Ute Mountain

CONNECTICUT

Mashantucket Pequot Council
P. O. Box 160
Ledyard, CT 06339
(203) 536-2681

FLORIDA

Miccosukee Business Committee
P. O. Box 44021
Tamiami Station
Miami, FL 33144
(305) 223-8380
Nation: Miccosukee-Creek

Seminole Tribal Council
6073 Stirling Rd.
Hollywood, FL 33024
(305) 583-7112
Nation: Seminole

IDAHO

Coeur d'Alene Tribal Council
Plummer, ID 83851
(208) 274-3101
Nation: Coeur d'Alene

Fort Hall Business Council
Fort Hall Tribal Office
Fort Hall, ID 83203
(208) 238-3700
Nation: Shoshone-Bannock

Kootenai Tribal Council
P. O. Box 1269
Bonners Ferry, ID 83805
(208) 267-3519
Nation: Kootenai

Nez Perce Executive Committee
P. O. Box 305
Lapwai, ID 83540
(208) 843-2253
Nation: Nez Perce

Northwestern Band of Shoshoni Nation Council
P. O. Box 145
Fort Hall, ID 83203
(208) 238-0916
Nation: Shoshoni

Summit Lake Paiute Council
P. O. Box 597
Fort Hall, ID 83203
(208) 237-6528
Nation: Summit Lake Paiute

IOWA

Sac & Fox Tribal Council
Rte. 2, P. O. Box 56C
Tama, IA 52339
(515) 484-4678
Nation: Sac and Fox

KANSAS

Iowa Executive Committee
Rte. 1, P. O. Box 58A
White Cloud, KS 66094
(913) 595-3258
Nation: Iowa of Kansas and Nebraska

Kickapoo Tribal Council
Rte. 1, P. O. Box 157A
Horton, KS 66439
(913) 486-2131
Nation: Kickapoo

Prairie Potawatomi
Tribal Council
P. O. Box 97
Mayetta, KS 66509
(913) 966-2255
Nation: Prairie Potawatomi

Sac and Fox Tribal Council
P. O. Box 38
Reserve, KS 66434
(913) 742-7471
Nation: Sac and Fox

LOUISANA

Chitimacha Tribal Council
P. O. Box 661
Charenton, LA 70523
(318) 923-4973
Nation: Chitimacha

Coushatta Tribal Council
P. O. Box 818
Elton, LA 70532
(318) 584-2261
Nation: Coushatta

Tunica-Biloxi Indian Tribe
P. O. Box 311
Mansura, LA 71351
(318) 253-9767

NATIONAL COUNCILS

MAINE

Houlton Maliseet Band Council
P. O. Box 576
Houlton, ME 04730
(207) 532-4273
Nation: Maliseet

Indian Township
Passamaquoddy Tribal Council
P. O. Box 301
Princeton, ME 04668
(207) 796-2301
Nation: Passamaquoddy

Penobscot Tribal Council
Six River Road Indian
Reservation
Old Town, ME 04468
(207) 827-7776
Nation: Penobscot

Pleasant Point Passamaquoddy
Tribal Council
P. O. Box 343
Perry, ME 04667
(207) 853-2551
Nation: Passamaquoddy

MASSACHUSETTS

Wampanoag Tribal Council of
Gay Head
RFD Box 137
Gay Head, MA 02535
(508) 645-9265
Nation: Wampanoag

MICHIGAN

Bay Mills Executive Council
Rte. 1
Brimley, MI 49715
(906) 248-3241
Nation: Chippewa

Grand Traverse Band
Tribal Council
Rte. 1, P. O. Box 135
Suttons Bay, MI 49682
(616) 271-3538
Nation: Chippewa

Hannahville Indian Community
Council
Hannahville Rte. 1
Road N14910
Wilson, MI 49896
(906) 466-2342
Nation: Potawatomi

Keweenaw Bay Tribal Council
Tribal Center Bldg.,
Rte. 1, P. O. Box 45
Baraga, MI 49908
(906) 353-6623
Nation: Chippewa

Lac Vieux Desert Band of
Chippewa Indians Council
P. O. Box 446
Watersmeet, MI 49969
(906) 358-4722
Nation: Chippewa

Saginaw-Chippewa
Tribal Council
7070 E. Broadway Rd.
Mt. Pleasant, MI 48858
(517) 772-5700
Nation: Saginaw-Chippewa

Sault Ste. Marie Chippewa
Tribal Council
206 Greenbough St..
Sault Ste. Marie, MI 49783
(906) 635-6050
Nation: Chippewa

MINNESOTA

Fond Du Lac Reservation
Business Committee
105 University Rd.
Cloquet, MN 55720
(218) 879-4593
Nation: Chippewa

Grand Portage Reservation
Business Committee
P. O. Box 428
Grand Portage, MN 55605
(218) 475-2279
Nation: Chippewa

Leech Lake Reservation
Business Committee
Rte. 3, P. O. Box 100
Cass Lake, MN 56633
(218) 335-2207
Nation: Chippewa

Lower Sioux Indian Community
Council
RR 1, P. O. Box 308
Morton, MN 56270
(507) 697-6185
Nation: Mdewakanton Sioux

Mille Lacs Reservation
Business Committee
Star Route
Onamia, MN 56359
(612) 532-4181
Nation: Chippewa

Minnesota Chippewa Tribal
Executive Committee
P. O. Box 217
Cass Lake, MN 56633
(218) 335-2252
Nation: Chippewa

Nett Lake Reservation (Bois
Fort Tribe) Business Committee
P. O. Box 16
Nett Lake, MN 55772
(218) 757-3261
Nation: Chippewa

Prairie Island Community
Council
5750 Sturgeon Lake Rd.
Welch, MN 55089
(612) 388-8889
Nation: Mdewakanton Sioux

Red Lake Tribal Council
P. O. Box 550
Red Lake, MN 56671
(218) 679-3341
Nation: Chippewa

Shakopee Sioux Community
Council
2330 Sioux Trail, NW
Prior Lake, MN 55372
(612) 445-8900
Nation: Mdewankanton Sioux

Upper Sioux Board of Trustees
P. O. Box 147
Granite Falls, MN 56241
(612) 564-2360
Nation: Santee Sioux

White Earth Reservation
Business Committee
P. O. Box 418
White Earth, MN 56591
(218) 983-3285
Nation: Chippewa

NATIONAL COUNCILS

MISSISSIPPI
Tribal Council of the Mississippi
Band of Choctaws
Rte. 7, P. O. Box 21
Philadelphia, MS 39350
(601) 656-5251
Nation: Choctaws

MISSOURI
Eastern Shawnee Tribal Council
P. O. Box 350
Seneca, MO 64865
(417) 776-2435
Nation: Eastern Shawnee

MONTANA
Blackfeet Tribal Business
Council
P. O. Box 850
Browning, MT 59417
(406) 338-7276
Nation: Blackfeet

Chippewa-Cree Business
Committee
P. O. Box Elder, MT 59521
(406) 395-4482
Nation: Chippewa and Cree

Confederated Salish and
Kootenai Tribal Council
P. O. Box 278
Pablo, MT 59855
(406) 675-2706
Nation: Salish and Kootenai

Crow Tribal Council
P. O. Box 159
Crow Agency, MT 59022
(406) 638-2316
Nation: Crow

Fort Belknap Community
Council
P. O. Box 249
Harlem, MT 59526
(406) 353-2205
Nation: Assiniboine Sioux and
Gros Ventre

Fort Peck Executive Board
P. O. Box 1027
Poplar, MT 59255
(406) 768-5311
Nation: Assiniboine Sioux

Northern Cheyenne Tribal
Council
P. O. Box 128
Lame Deer, MT 59043
(406) 477-6284
Nation: Northern Cheyenne

NEBRASKA
Omaha Tribal Council
P. O. Box 368
Macy, NE 68039
(402) 837-5391
Nation: Omaha

Ponca Tribe of Nebraska
3610 Dodge St.
Omaha, NE 68131
(402) 342-4814
Nation: Ponca

Santee Sioux Tribal Council
Rte. 2
Niobrara, NE 68760
(402) 857-3302
Nation: Santee Sioux

Winnebago Tribal Council
Winnebago, NE 68071
(402) 878-2272
Nation: Winnebago

NEVADA
Battle Mountain Band Council
P. O. Box 578
Battle Mountain, NV 89820
(702) 635-2004
Nation: Te-Moak Band

Carson Colony Community
Council
502 Shoshone St.
Carson City, NV 89701
(702) 883-6431
Nation: Washoe

Dresslerville Community
Council
P. O. Box 2087
Gardnerville, NV 89410
(702) 265-4191
Nation: Washoe

Duckwater Shoshone
Tribal Council
P. O. Box 68
Duckwater, NV 89314
(702) 863-0227
Nation: Shoshone

Elko Band Council
P. O. Box 748
Elko, NV 89801
(702) 738-8869
Nation: Te-Moak Band

Ely Colony Council
16 Shoshone Circle
Ely, NV 89801
(702) 289-3013
Nation: Shoshone

Fallon Business Council
8955 Mission Rd.
Fallon, NV 89406
(702) 423-6075
Nation: Paiute and Shoshone

Fort McDermitt Tribal Council
P. O. Box 457
McDermitt, NV 89421
(702) 532-8259
Nation: Paiute and Shoshone

Las Vegas Colony Council
No 1 Paiute Dr.
Las Vegas, NV 89106
(702) 386-3926
Nation: Paiute

Lovelock Tribal Council
P. O. Box 878
Lovelock, NV 89419
(702) 273-7861
Nation: Paiute

Moapa Business Council
P. O. Box 56
Las Vegas, NV 89025
(702) 865-2787
Nation: Moapa Band of Paiute
Indians

Pyramid Lake Paiute
Tribal Council
P. O. Box 256
Nixon, NV 89424
(702) 574-0140
Nation: Paiute

Reno-Sparks Indian Council
98 Colony Rd.
Reno, NV 89502
(702) 329-2936
Nation: Washoe and Paiute

NATIONAL COUNCILS

Shoshone-Paiute Business
Council
P. O. Box 219
Owyhee, NV 89832
(702) 757-3161
Nation: Shoshone and Paiute

South Fork Band Council
P. O. Box B-13
Lee, NV 89829
(702) 744-4273
Nation: Te-Moak Band

Summit Lake Paiute Council
P. O. Box 1958
Winnemucca, NV 89445
(702) 623-5151
Nation: Paiute

Te-Moak Tribal Council
525 Sunset St.
Elko, NV 89801
(702) 738-9251
Nation: Te-Moak Band

Walker River Paiute
Tribal Council
P. O. Box 220
Schurz, NV 89427
(702) 773-2306
Nation: Paiute

Washoe Tribal Council
919 Highway 395 South
Gardnerville, NV 89410
(702) 265-4191
Nation: Washoe

Wells Indian Colony
Band Council
P. O. Box 809
Wells, NV 89835
(702) 752-3045
Nation: Te-Moak Band

Yerington Paiute Tribal Council
171 Campbell Lane
Yerington, NV 89447
(702) 463-3301
Nation: Paiute

Yomba Tribal Council
Rte. 1, P. O. Box 24
Austin, NV 89310
(702) 964-2463
Nation: Shoshone

NEW MEXICO

Acoma Pueblo Council
P. O. Box 309
Acomita, NM 87034
(505) 552-6604
Nation: Pueblo

Cochiti Pueblo Council
P. O. Box 70
Cochiti, NM 87041
(505) 465-2244
Nation: Pueblo

Isleta Pueblo Council
P. O. Box 317
Isleta, NM 87022
(505) 869-3111
Nation: Pueblo

Jemez Pueblo Council
P. O. Box 78
Jemez, NM 87024
(505) 834-7359
Nation: Pueblo

Jicarilla Apache Tribal Council
P. O. Box 147
Dulce, NM 87528
(505) 759-3242
Nation: Jicarilla Apache

Laguna Pueblo Council
P. O. Box 194
Laguna, NM 87026
(505) 552-6654
Nation: Pueblo

Mescalero Apache
Tribal Council
P. O. Box 176
Mescalero, NM 87340
(505) 671-4495
Nation: Mescalero Apache

Nambe Pueblo Council
Rte. 1, P. O. Box 117-BB
Santa Fe, NM 87501
(505) 455-7752
Nation: Pueblo

Picuris Pueblo Council
P. O. Box 127
Penasco, NM 87553
(505) 587-2519
Nation: Pueblo

Pojoaque Pueblo Council
Rte. 11, P. O. Box 71
Santa Fe, NM 87501
(505) 455-2278
Nation: Pueblo

Ramah Navajo Chapter Council
P. O. Box 267
Ramah, NM 81137
(505) 775-3383
Nation: Navajo

San Felipe Pueblo Council
P. O. Box A
San Felipe Pueblo, NM 87001
(505) 867-3381
Nation: Pueblo

San Ildefonso Pueblo Council
Rte. 5, P. O. Box 315-A
Santa Fe, NM 87501
(505) 455-2273
Nation: Pueblo

San Juan Pueblo Council
P. O. Box 1099
San Juan Pueblo, NM 87566
(505) 852-4400
Nation: Pueblo

Sandia Pueblo Tribal Council
P. O. Box 6008
Bernalillo, NM 87004
(505) 867-3317
Nation: Pueblo

Santa Ana Pueblo Council
P. O. Box 37
Bernalillo, NM 87004
(505) 867-3301
Nation: Pueblo

Santa Clara Pueblo Council
P. O. Box 580
Espanola, NM 87532
(505) 753-7330
Nation: Pueblo

Santo Domingo Pueblo Council
P. O. Box 99
Santo Domingo, NM 87052
(505) 465-2214
Nation: Pueblo

Taos Pueblo Council
P. O. Box 1846
Taos, NM 87571
(505) 758-9593
Nation: Pueblo

NATIONAL COUNCILS

Tesuque Pueblo Council
Rte. 11, P. O. Box 1
Santa Fe, NM 87501
(505) 983-2667
Nation: Pueblo

Zia Tribal Council
General Delivery
San Ysidro, NM 87053
(505) 867-3304
Nation: Pueblo

Zuni Pueblo Tribal Council
P. O. Box 339
Zuni, NM 87327
(505) 782-4481
Nation: Pueblo

NEW YORK

Cayuga Nation Tribal Council
P. O. Box 11
Versailles, NY 14168
(716) 532-4847
Nation: Cayuga

Oneida Nation Tribal Council
Rte. 2, West Rd.
Oneida, NY 13424
Nation: Oneida

Onondaga Nation
Tribal Council
P. O. Box 319B
Nedrow, NY 13120
(716) 469-7810
Nation: Onondaga

St. Regis Mohawk
Tribal Council
St. Regis Reservation
Hogansburg, NY 13655
(518) 358-2272
Nation: St. Regis Mohawk

Seneca Nation Tribal Council
P. O. Box 231
Salamanca, NY 14779
(716) 532-4900
Nation: Seneca

Tonawanda Band of Senecas
Council of Chiefs
7027 Meadville Rd.
Basom, NY 14013
(716) 542-9942
Nation: Seneca

Tuscarora Nation Tribal Council
2006 Mt. Hope Rd.
Lewiston, NY 14092
(716) 297-4990
Nation: Tuscarora

NORTH CAROLINA

Cherokee (Eastern Band)
Tribal Council
P. O. Box 455
Cherokee, NC 28719
(704) 497-2771
Nation: Cherokee

NORTH DAKOTA

Devil's Lake Sioux
Tribal Council
Sioux Community Center
Fort Totten, ND 58335
(701) 766-4221
Nation: Sisseton-Wahpeton Sioux

Fort Berthold Tribal Business
Council
P. O. Box 220
Tribal Administration Bldg.
New Town, ND 58763
(701) 627-4781
Nation: Mandan, Hidasta and Arikara

Standing Rock Sioux
Tribal Council
Fort Yates, ND 58538
(701) 854-7231
Nation: Standing Rock Sioux

Turtle Mountain Tribal Council
Belcourt, ND 58316
(701) 477-6451
Nation: Chippewa

OKLAHOMA

Absentee-Shawnee Executive
Committee
P. O. Box 1747
Shawnee, OK 74801
(405) 275-4030
Nation: Absentee-Shawnee

Alabama-Quassarte Tribal
Town Council
P. O. Box 404
Eufaula, OK 74432
(918) 689-9570
Nation: Creek

Apache Business Committee
P. O. Box 1220
Anadarko, OK 73005
(405) 247-9493
Nation: Apache

Caddo Tribal Council
P. O. Box 487
Binger, OK 73009
(405) 656-2344
Nation: Caddo

Cherokee Tribal Council
P. O. Box 948
Tahlequah, OK 74465
(918) 456-0671
Nation: Cherokee

Cheyenne-Arapaho Business
Committee
P. O. Box 38
Concho, OK 73022
(405) 262-0345
Nation: Cheyenne and Arapaho

Chickasaw Tribal Legislature
P. O. Box 2669
Ada, OK 74820
(405) 436-1460
Nation: Chickasaw

Choctaw Tribal Council
P.O. Drawer 1210
16th and Locust Sts.
Durant, OK 74701
(405) 924-8280
Nation: Choctaw

Citizen Band Potawatomi
Business Committee
P. O. Box 151
Shawnee, OK 74801
(405) 275-3125
Nation: Potawatomi

Comanche Tribal Business
Committee
P. O. Box 908
Lawton, OK 73502
(405) 247-3444
Nation: Comanche

Delaware
Executive Committee
P. O. Box 825
Anadarko, OK 73005
(405) 247-2448
Nation: Delaware

NATIONAL COUNCILS

Fort Sill Apache Business
Committee
Rte. 2, P. O. Box 121
Apache, OK 73006
(405) 588-2298
Nation: Apache

Iowa of Oklahoma Business
Committee
Iowa Veterans Hall
P. O. Box 190
Perkins, OK 74059
Nation: Iowa

Kaw Business Committee
Drawer 50
Kaw City, OK 74641
(405) 269-2552
Nation: Kaw

Kialagee Tribal Town
928 Alex Noon Dr.
Wetumpka, OK 74883
Nation: Creek

Kickapoo of Oklahoma
Business Committee
P. O. Box 58
McLoud, OK 74851
(405) 964-2075
Nation: Kickapoo

Kiowa Business Committee
P. O. Box 369
Carnegie, OK 73015
(405) 654-2300
Nation: Kiowa

Miami Business Committee
P. O. Box 636
Miami, OK 74355
(918) 540-2890
Nation: Miami

Modoc Tribal Council
P. O. Box 939
Miami, OK 74354
(918) 542-1190
Nation: Modoc

Muskogee (Creek)
National Council
P. O. Box 580
Okmulgee, OK
(918) 756-8700
Nation: Muskogee

Osage Tribal Council
Tribal Administration Bldg.
Pawhuska, OK 74056
(918) 287-4622
Nation: Osage

Otoe-Missouria Tribal Council
P. O. Box 68
Red Rock, OK 74058
(405) 723-4434
Nation: Otoe and Missouria

Ottawa Business Council
P. O. Box 110
Miami, OK 74355
(918) 540-1536
Nation: Ottawa

Pawnee Business Committee
P. O. Box 470
Pawnee, OK 74058
(918) 540-2535
Nation: Peoria

Peoria Council
P. O. Box 1527
Miami, OK 74355
(918) 540-2535
Nation: Peoria

Ponca Business Committee
P. O. Box 2, White Eagle
Ponca City, OK 74601
(405) 762-8104
Nation: Ponca

Quapaw Tribal Business
Committee
P. O. Box 765
Quapaw, OK 74363
(918) 542-1853
Nation: Quapaw

Sac & Fox of Oklahoma
Business Committee
Rte. 2, P. O. Box 246
Stroud, OK 74049
(918) 968-3526
Nation: Sac and Fox

Seminole General Council
P. O. Box 1495
Wewoka, OK 74884
(405) 258-6287
Nation: Seminole

Seneca-Cayuga Business
Committee
P. O. Box 1283
Miami, OK 74355
(918) 542-6609
Nation: Seneca and Cayuga

Thlopthlocco Tribal Town
Business Committee
Rte. 2, P. O. Box 204
Wetumka, OK 74883
(405) 452-3529
Nation: Creek

Tonkawa Business Committee
P. O. Box 70
Tonkawa, OK 74653
(405) 628-2561
Nation: Tonkawa

United Keetoowah Cherokee
Council
2450 S. Muskogee Ave.
Tahlequah, OK 74464
(918) 456-5491
Nation: Cherokee

Wichita Executive Committee
P. O. Box 729
Anadarko, OK 73005
(405) 247-2425
Nation: Wichita

Wyandotte Business
Committee
P. O. Box 250
Wyandotte, OK 74370
(918) 678-2297
Nation: Wyandotte

OREGON

Burns-Paiute General Council
HC 71, 100 Pa Si Go St
Burns, OR 97720
(503) 573-2088
Nation: Burns Paiute

Confederated Tribes of Coos
Lower Umpqua & Suislaw
Indians Tribal Council
455 South 4th St
Coos Bay, OR 97420
(503) 267-5454

NATIONAL COUNCILS

Confederated Tribes of the
Grande Ronde Indian
Community Council
P. O. Box 38
Grande Ronda, OR 97347
(503) 879-5215

Cow Creek Band of Umpqua
Indians Community Council
649 W. Harrison
Roseburg, OR 97470
(503) 672-9405

Klamath General Council
P. O. Box 436
Chiloquin, OR 97624
(503) 783-2219

Northwestern Band of
Shoshoni Business Council
Cow Creek Tribal Office
2400 Stewart Pky. #300
Roseburg, OR 97470
Nation: Shoshoni

Siletz Tribal Council
P. O. Box 549
Siletz, OR 97380
(503) 444-2528

Umatilla Board of Trustees
P. O. Box 638
Pendleton, OR 97801
(503) 276-3165
Nation: Umatilla

Warm Springs Tribal Council
P. O. Box C
Warm Springs, OR 97761
(503) 553-1161
Nation: Walla Walla and
Cayuga

RHODE ISLAND

Narragansett Indian
Tribal Council
P. O. Box 268
Charleston, RI 02813
(401) 364-110

SOUTH DAKOTA

Cheyenne River Sioux
Tribal Council
P. O. Box 590
Eagle Butte, SD 57625
(605) 964-4155
Nation: Cheyenne River Sioux

Crow Creek Sioux
Tribal Council
P. O. Box 50
Fort Thompson, SD 57339
(605) 245-2221
Nation: Crow Creek Sioux

Flandreau Santee-Sioux
Executive Committee
Flandreau Field Office
P. O. Box 283
Flandreau, SD 57028
(605) 997-3891
Nation: Santee Sioux

Lower Brule Sioux
Tribal Council
Lower Brule, SD 57548
(605) 473-5561
Nation: Lower Brule Sioux

Oglala Sioux Tribal Council
Pine Ridge, SD 57770
(605) 867-5821
Nation: Oglala Sioux

Rosebud Sioux Tribal Council
Rosebud, SD 57570
(605) 747-2381
Nation: Rosebud Sioux

Sisseton-Wahpeton Sioux
Tribal Council
Rte. 2, Agency Village
Sisseton, SD 57262
(605) 698-3911
Nation: Sisseton-Wahpeton
Sioux

Standing Rock Sioux
Tribal Council
Fort Yates, ND 58538
(701) 854-7231
Nation: Standing Rock Sioux

Yankton Sioux Tribal Business
& Claims Committee
P. O. Box 248
Marty, SD 57361
Nation: Yankton Sioux

TEXAS

Alabama-Coushatta
Tribal Council
Rte. 3, P. O. Box 640
Livingston, TX 77351
(409) 563-4391

Tigua Ysleta Del Sur Council
119 S. Old Pueblo Rd.
P. O. Box 17579
El Paso, TX 79907
Nation: Pueblo

UTAH

Goshute Business Council
P. O. Box 6104
Ibapah, UT 84034
(801) 234-1138
Nation: Goshute

Paiute Tribal Council
600 North 100 East
Cedar City, UT 84720
(801) 586-1112
Nation: Paiute

Skull Valley Executive
Community
Bureau of Indian Affairs
Fort Duchesne, UT 84026
(801) 722-2406
Nation: Goshute

Uintah and Ouray
Tribal Business Council
Fort Duchesne, UT 84026
(801) 722-5141
Nation: Ute

VIRGINIA

Pamunkey Tribal Government
RR 1, P. O. Box 2225
King William, VA 23086
(804) 843-3526

WASHINGTON

Chehalis Community Council
P. O. Box 536
Oakville, WA 998568
(206) 273-5911
Nation: Chehalis

Colville Business Committee
P. O. Box 150
Nespelem, WA 99155
(509) 634-4711
Nation: Colville

Hoh Tribal Business Committee
HC 80, P. O. Box 917
Forks, WA 98331
(206) 374-6582
Nation: Hoh

NATIONAL COUNCILS

Jamestown Band of Klallem
Indians Business Council
305 Old Blyn Highway
Sequim, WA 98382
(206) 683-1109
Nation: Klallem

Kalispel Business Committee
P. O. Box 39
Usk, WA 99180
(509) 445-1147
Nation: Kalispel

Lower Elwha Community
Council
1666 Lower Elwha Community
Center
Port Angeles, WA 98362
(206) 452-8471
Nation: Klallem

Lummi Indian Business Council
2616 Kwina Rd
Bellingham, WA 98226
(206) 734-8180
Nation: Lummi

Makah Tribal Council
P. O. Box 115
Neah Bay, WA 98357
(206) 645-2205
Nation: Makah

Muckleshoot Tribal Council
39016 172nd St. SE
Auburn, WA 98002
(206) 939-3311
Nation: Muckleshoot

Nisqually Indian Community
Council
4820 She Na-Num Dr., S. E.
Olympia, WA 98503
(206) 456-5221
Nation: Nisqually

Nooksack Tribal Council
P. O. Box 157
Deming, WA 98244
(206) 592-5276
Nation: Nooksack

Port Gamble Community
Council
P. O. Box 280
Kingston, WA 98346
(206) 297-2646
Nation: Klallm

Puyallup Tribal Council
2002 East 28th St.
Tacoma, WA 98404
(206) 597-6200
Nation: Puyallup

Quileute Tribal Council
P. O. Box 279
LaPush, WA 98350
(206) 374-6163
Nation: Quileute

Quinault Business Committee
P. O. Box 189
Taholah, WA 98587
(206) 276-8211
Nation: Quinault

Sauk-Suiattle Tribal Council
5318 Chief Brown Line
Darrington, WA 98241
(206) 435-8366
Nation: Sauk-Suiattle

Shoalwater Bay Tribal Council
P. O. Box 130
Takeland, WA 98590
(206) 267-6766
Nation: Shoalwater

Skokmish Tribal Council
No. 80 Tribal Center Rd.
Shelton, WA 98584
(206) 426-4232
Nation: Skokomish

Spokane Business Council
P. O. Box 100
Wellpinit, WA 99040
(509) 258-4581
Nation: Spokane

Squaxin Island Tribal Council
West 81 Highway 108
Shelton, WA 98584
(206) 426-9781
Nation: Squaxin Island

Stillaquamish Board of
Directors
3439 Stoluckquamish Lane
Arlington, WA 98223
(206) 652-7362
Nation: Stillaguamish

Suquamish Tribal Council
P. O. Box 498
Suquamish, WA 98392
(206) 598-3311
Nation: Suquamish

Swinomish Indian Senate
P. O. Box 817
LaConnor, WA 98257
(206) 466-3163
Nation: Swinomish

Tulalip Board of Directors
6700 Totem Beach Rd.
Marysville, WA 98279
(206) 653-4585
Nation: Tulalip

Upper Skagit Tribal Council
2284 Community Plaza
Sedro Wooley, WA 98284
(206) 856-5501
Nation: Skagit

Yakima Tribal Council
P. O. Box 151
Toppenish, WA 98948
(509) 865-5121
Nation: Yakima

WISCONSIN

Bad River Tribal Council
Rte. 39
Odanah, WI 54861
(715) 682-4212
Nation: Chippewa

Forest County Potawatomi
General Council
P. O. Box 346
Crandon, WI 54520
(715) 478-2903
Nation: Potawatomi

Lac Courte Oreilles
Tribal Governing Board
Rte. 2, P. O. Box 2700
Hayward, WI 54843
(715) 634-8934
Nation: Chippewa

Lac du Flambeau Tribal Council
P. O. Box 67
Lac du Flambeau, WI 54538
(715) 588-3303
Nation: Chippewa

NATIONAL COUNCILS

Menominee Tribal Legislature
P. O. Box 397
Keshena, WI 54135
(715) 799-3341
Nation: Menominee

Oneida Executive Committee
P. O. Box 365
Oneida, WI 54155
(414) 869-2772
Nation: Oneida

Red Cliff Tribal Council
P. O. Box 529
Bayfield, WI 54814
(715) 779-5805
Nation: Chippewa

St. Croix Council
P. O. Box 287
Hertel, WI 54845
(715) 349-2195
Nation: Chippewa

Sokaogon Chippewa
Tribal Council
Rte. 1, P. O. Box 625
Crandon, WI 54520
(715) 478-3543
Nation: Chippewa

Stockbridge-Munsee
Tribal Council
Rte. 1
Bowler, WI 54416
(715) 793-4111
Nation: Mohican

Wisconsin Winnebago
Business Council
P. O. Box 311
Tomah, WI 54660
(608) 372-4147
Nation: Winnebago

WYOMING

Shoshone & Arapaho Joint
Tribal Business Council
P. O. Box 308
Fort Washakie, WY 82514
(307) 332-7163
Nation: Wind River Shoshone
 & Arapaho

BUREAU OF INDIAN AFFAIRS

The Bureau of Indian Affairs is the government agency charged with overseeing tribal matters. The offices are listed regionally. The primary office is in Washington D.C.

Central Office:
Bureau of Indian Affairs
Department of the Interior
1849 C St. NW
Washington, DC 20245
(202) 208-3711

Area Offices:

Aberdeen Area Office:
Bureau of Indian Affairs
Federal Building
115 4th Ave. SE
Aberdeen, SD 57401
(605) 226-7261
Administers programs for regions of North and South Dakota, and Nebraska.

Albuquerque Area Office:
Bureau of Indian Affairs
P.O. Box 26567
Albuquerque, NM 87125-6567
(505) 766-3170
Administers programs for regions of Colorado and New Mexico.

Anadarko Area Office:
Bureau of Indian Affairs
W.C.D. Office Complex,
Box 368
Anadarko, OK 73005
(405) 247-6673
Administers programs for regions of Western Oklahoma, Kansas, and Missouri.

Billings Area Office:
Bureau of Indian Affairs
316 North 26th St.
Billings, MT 59101
(406) 657-6315
Administers programs for regions of Montana and Wyoming.

Eastern Area Office:
Bureau of Indian Affairs
1951 Constitution Ave. NW
MS 260-Broyhill Building
Washington, D.C. 20245
(703) 235-3006
Administers programs for regions in states east of the Mississippi River.

Juneau Area Office:
Bureau of Indian Affairs
P.O. Box 3-8000
Federal Building
Juneau, AK 99802
(907) 586-7177
Administers programs within the State of Alaska.

Minneapolis Area Office:
Bureau of Indian Affairs
331 2nd Ave. S
Minneapolis, MN 55401-2241
(612) 373-1000
Administers programs for regions of Iowa, Michigan, Minnesota, and Wisconsin.

Muskogee Area Office:
Bureau of Indian Affairs
Old Federal Building
Muskogee, OK 74401
(918) 687-2296
Administers programs for regions of Eastern Oklahoma.

Navajo Area Office:
Bureau of Indian Affairs
P.O. Box M
Window Rock, AZ 86515
(602) 871-5151
Administers Navajo programs in Arizona, New Mexico and Utah.

Phoenix Area Office:
Bureau of Indian Affairs
P.O. Box 10, 1 N. First St.
Phoenix, AZ 85001
(602) 379-6600
Administers programs for regions of Arizona, California, Nevada, and Utah.

Portland Area Office:
Bureau of Indian Affairs
Federal Building
1002 NE Holladay St.
Portland, OR 97232-4182
(503) 231-6702
Administers programs for regions of Oregon, Washington, and Idaho.

Sacramento Area Office:
Bureau of Indian Affairs
Federal Office Building
2800 Cottage Way
Sacramento, CA 95825
(916) 978-4691
Administers programs within the State of California.

STATE INDIAN COMMISSIONS

I ndividual states have developed commissions to address American Indian issues.

ALABAMA
Alabama Indian Affairs Commission
339 Dexter Ave., Suite 113
Suite 113
Montgomery, AL 36130

ALASKA
Assistant for Alaska Native Affairs
Office of the Governor
Pouch A
Juneau, AK 99811

ARIZONA
Arizona Commission on Indian Affairs
1645 W. Jefferson
Suite 433
Phoenix, AZ 85007

CALIFORNIA
California Native American Heritage Commission
915 Capitol Mall
Sacramento, CA 95814

COLORADO
Colorado Commission of Indian Affairs
130 State Capitol
Denver, CO 80203

CONNECTICUT
Connecticut Indian Affairs Council
Department of Environmental Protection
165 Capitol Ave.
Hartford, CT 06106

DELAWARE
Office of Human Relations
630 State College Rd.
Dover, DE 19901

FLORIDA
Florida Governor's Council on Indian Affairs
521 E. College Ave.
Tallahassee, FL 32301

GEORGIA
Office of Indian Heritage
330 Capitol Ave. SE
Atlanta, Ga 30334

HAWAII
Hawaii Council of American Indian Nations
Box 17627
910 N. Vineyard Blvd.
Honolulu, HI 96817

IDAHO
American Indian Coordinator
State House
Boise, ID 83720

IOWA
Office of the Governor
State Capitol
Des Moines, IA 50319

LOUISANA
Governor's Commission on Indian Affairs
Box 44455, Capitol Station
Baton Rouge, LA 70804

MAINE
Maine Indian Affairs Commission
State Health Station #38
Augusta, ME 04333

MARYLAND
Commission on Indian Affairs
45 Calvert St.
Annapolis, MD 21401

MASSACHUSETTS
Massachusetts Commission on Indian Affairs
One Ashburn PL., Rm 1004
Boston, MA 02108

MICHIGAN
Michigan Commission on Indian Affairs
Dept. of Management and Budget
Box 30026
611 W. Ottawa St.
Lansing, MI 48909

MINNESOTA
MN Council on Indian Affairs
127 University Ave.
St. Paul, MN 55155

MONTANA
Governor's Office of Indian Affairs
1218 E. Sixth Ave.
Helena, MT 59620

NEBRASKA
Nebraska Indian Commission
Box 94914, State Capitol
Lincoln, NE 68701

STATE INDIAN COMMISSIONS

NEVADA
Nevada Indian Commission
3100 Mill St., Suite 206
Reno, NV 89502

NEW HAMPSHIRE
New Hampshire Indian Council
913 Elm St.
Room 201
Manchester, NH 03101

NEW JERSEY
New Jersey Indian Office
300 Main St., Suite 3F
Orange, NJ 07050

NEW MEXICO
New Mexico Office on Indian Affairs
La Villa Rivera Building
Santa Fe, NM 87501

NEW YORK
Dept. of Indian Services
Donovan State Office Bldg.
125 Main St., Rm 471
Buffalo, NY 14203

NORTH CAROLINA
North Carolina Commission on Indian Affairs
Box 27228
227 E. Edenton St. #229
Raleigh, NC 27611

NORTH DAKOTA
North Dakota Indian Affairs Commission
State Capitol Bldg.
Bismarck, ND 58505

OHIO
Ohio Indian Affairs Coordinator
Outdoor Recreation Service
Fountain Square Bldg. E
Columbus, OH 43224

OKLAHOMA
Oklahoma Indian Affairs Commission
4010 N. Lincoln
Oklahoma City, OK 73105

OREGON
Commission on Indian Affairs
454 State Capitol Bldg.
Salem, OR 97310

RHODE ISLAND
Rhode Island Commission for Indian Affairs
444 Friendship St.
Providence, RI 02907

SOUTH CAROLINA
Assistant to the Governor
Box 11450
Columbia, SC 29211

SOUTH DAKOTA
South Dakota Office of Indian Affairs
Kneip Bldg.
Pierre, SD 57501

TEXAS
Texas Indian Commission
Box 2960
Austin, TX 78768

TENNESSEE
Tennessee Indian Council
1110 12th Ave. S.
Nashville, TN 30273

UTAH
Utah Divison of Indian Affairs
6220 State Office Bldg.
Salt Lake City, UT 84114

VIRGINIA
Indian Affairs Coordinator
Secretary of Human Resources
9th Street Office Bldg., Rm 622
Richmond, VA 23219

WASHINGTON
Washington Commission for Indian Affairs
1057 Capitol Way
Olympia, WA 98504

WISCONSIN
Wisconsin Governor's Indian Desk
Box 7863
Madison, WI 53701

WYOMING
Wyoming State Indian Commission
2660 Peck Ave.
Riverton, WY 82501

URBAN INDIAN SERVICE PROJECTS

O rganizations, both urban and on the reservation, that are concerned with American Indian affairs.

ALASKA
Alaska Federation of Natives
411 W. 4th Ave., Suite 1A
Anchorage, AK 99501

Alaska Native Brotherhood
P. O. Box 72
Sitka, AK 99835

Alaska Native Foundation
733 W. 4th #202
Anchorage, AK 99501

Fairbanks Native Association
310 1/2 First Ave.
Fairbanks, AK 99710

Institute of Alaska Native Art
P. O. Box 80583
Fairbanks, AK 99708

ARIZONA
Affiliation of Arizona Indian Centers
2721 N. Central, Suite 910
Phoenix, AZ 85004

American Indian Consultants
2070 E. Southern Ave.
Tempe, AZ 85282

Community Conference Center
1015 E. 2nd St.
Winslow, AZ 86047

Indian Development District of Arizona
1777 W. Camelback Rd.
Suite A-108
Phoenix, AZ 85015

Inter-Tribal Council of Arizona
124 W. Thomas Rd.
Suite 201
Phoenix, AZ 85013

Native Americans for Community Action
15 N. San Francisco St.
P. O. Box 572
Flagstaff, AZ 86001

National American Indian Housing Council
P. O. Box 776
Sells, AZ 85634

National Council of BIA Educators
P. O. Box 5
Tuba City, AZ 86045

National Indian Athletic Association
P. O. Box 645
315 N 24th St., #207-C
Phoenix, AZ 85001

Phoenix Indian Center
1337 N. First St.
Phoenix, AZ 85004

Tucson American Indian Association
P. O. Box 7246
Tucson, AZ 85725

United Indian Missions
P. O. Box U
2920 N 3rd St.
Flagstaff, AZ 86002

Winslow Indian Center
110 E. Second St.
Winslow, AZ 86047

Yuma Indian Center
670 E. 32nd St.
Yuma, AZ 85365

ARKANSAS
American Indian Center of Arkansas
309 State
Little Rock, AR 72201

Order of the Indian Wars
P. O. Box 7401
Little Rock, AR 72217

CALIFORNIA
American Indian Council of Central California
P. O. Box 3341
Bakerfield, CA 93385

American Indian Free Clinic
1173 South Hoover St.
Los Angeles, CA 90006

American Indian Historical Society
1451 Masonic Ave.
San Francisco, CA 94117

American Indian Training Program
319 MacArthur Blvd.
Oakland, CA 94610

Comprehensive Indian Rehabilitation Program
3621 N. Parkway Dr.
Frenso, CA 93711

Four Winds Lodge
1565 E. Santa Clara St.
San Jose, CA 95116

Fresno American Indian Council
5150 N 6th, #169
Fresno, CA 93710

URBAN INDIAN SERVICE PROJECTS

Friendship House
80 Julian Ave.
San Francisco, CA 94103

Indian Action Council
P. O. Box 1287
Eureka, CA 95501

Indian Center Inc.
1151 W. 6th St.
Los Angeles, CA 90017

Indian Center West
4840 S. Sepulveda Blvd.
Culver City, CA 92230

Inter-Tribal Council of California
1314 H St., Suite 100
Sacarmento, CA 95814

Inter-Tribal Friendship House
523 E. 14th Ave.
Oakland, CA 94606

Mendocino County Indian Center
1621 Talmage Rd.
Ukaih, CA 95482

Mi-Pi-Sho Development Center
210 Clay St.
P. O. Box 297
Independence, CA 93526

Native American Alcoholism and Drug Abuse Program
1815 39th Ave. #A
Oakland, CA 94601

National Indian Counselors Association Center for Counseling Service and Placement
San Diego State University
San Diego, CA 92182

Orange County Indian Center
12511 Brookhurts St.
Garden Grove, CA 92643

Sacramento Indian Center Alcoholism Awareness Program
1409 32nd St.
Sacramento, CA 95816

San Francisco Indian Center
225 Valencia
San Francisco, CA 94103

San Jose Indian Center
3485 E. Hills Dr.
San Jose, CA 95127

Seventh Generation Fund for Indian Development
P. O. Box 10
Forestville, CA 95436

United American Indian Involvement
118 Winston St.
Los Angeles, Ca 90013

United Indian Development Association
1541 Wilshire Blvd., Suite 418
Los Angeles, CA 90017

United Indian Lodge
1116 9th St.
Eureka, CA 95501

COLORADO

American Indian Science and Engineering Society
1310 College Ave., Suite 1220
Boulder, CO 80302

Colorado Indian Employment Assistance Center
P. O. Box 10134
University Park Station
Denver, CO 80210

Council of Energy Resource Tribes
1580 Logan St., Suite 400
Denver, CO 80203

Denver Indian Center
4407 Morrison Rd.
Denver, CO 80219

Denver Indian Health Board
2035 E. 18th Ave.
Denver, CO 80206

Eagle Lodge American Indian Alcoholism Rehabilitation Program
1264 Race St.
Denver, CO 80206

Institute for Indian Development
P. O. Box 1263
3575 S. Fox
Englewood, CO 80150

Inter-Tribal Heritage Project
3401 Pecos St.
Denver, CO 80211

National Council for Indian Business
10134 University Park Station
Denver, CO 80210

National Indian Health Board
1602 S. Parker Rd., Suite 200
Denver, CO 80231

National Indian Law Library
1506 Broadway
Boulder, CO 80302

National Indian Traders Association
P. O. Box 1263
3575 S. Fox
Englewood, CO 80150

National Urban Indian Council
1507 Broadway
Denver, CO 80120

Native American Rights Fund
1506 Broadway
Boulder, CO 80302

CONNECTICUT

American Indian Archaeological
Rte. 199, P. O. Box 260
Washington, CT 06793

American Indians for Development
P. O. Box 117
Meridan, CT 06450

DISTRICT OF COLUMBIA

American Indian Higher Education Consortium
333 Pennyslvania SE
Washington, DC 20003

American Indian National Bank
Commerce Bank Bldg., Suite 2000
1700 K ST. NW
Washington, DC 20006

URBAN INDIAN SERVICE PROJECTS

Americans for Indian
Opportunity
1140 Connecticut Ave. NW,
Suite 301
Washington, DC 20036

Bureau of Catholic Indian
Missions
20121 H St. NW
Washington, DC 20006

Indian Law Resource Center
601 E. Street SE
Washington, DC 20003

Institute for the Development of
Indian Law
927 15th St. NW, Suite 200
Washington, DC 20037

Interagency Task Force
American Indian Women
DOL-200 Constitution Ave. NW
Washington, DC 20201

Phelps-Stokes Fund
228 M Street NW
Washington, DC 20005

National American Indian Court
Judges Association
1000 Connecticut, Suite 401
Washington, DC 20036

National Congress of American
Indians
804 D Street NE
Washington, DC 20002

National Tribal Chairmen's
Association
918 18th St. NW, Suite 420
Washington, DC 20006

Native American Consultants
725 2nd St. NE
Washington, DC 20002

HAWAII

American Indian Services
Corporation
810 N. Vineyard Blvd.
Honolulu, HI 96819

Hawaii Council of American
Indian Nations
810 N. Vineyard Blvd.
Honolulu, HI 96817

ILLINOIS

American Indian Center
1630 W. Wilson
Chicago, IL 60640

Native American Committee
1628 W. Belmont
Chicago, IL 60657

National Indian Lutheran Board
35 E. Wacker Dr., Suite 1847
Chicago, IL 60601

St. Augustine Center for
American Indian
4512 N. Sheridan Blvd.
Chicago, IL 60640

IOWA

Indian Youth of America
P. O. Box 2786
4509 Stone Ave.
Sioux City, IA 51106

KANSAS

Lawrence Indian Center
P. O. Box 1016
Lawrence, KS 66044

Mid-America All Indian Center
650 N. Seneca
Wichita, KS 67203

MAINE

Central Maine Indian
Association
95 Main St.
Orono, ME 04473

Tribal Governors
93 Maine St.
Orono, ME 04473

MARYLAND

Baltimore American Indian
Center
113 S. Broadway
Baltimore, MD 21231

Boston Indian Council
105 S. Huntington Ave.
Jamaica Plain, MA 02130

Maryland Indian Council
P. O. Box 13161
Baltimore, MD 21203

North American Indian
Women's Association
10312 Folk Street
Silver Springs, MD 20902

MICHIGAN

All Tribe Indian Center
118 W. Pine St.
Ironwood, MI 39938

American Indian Community
Leadership Council
5315 Ravenswood RD.
Port Huron, MI 48060

Genesee Valley Indian
Association
124 W. 1st St.
Flint, MI 48502

Grand Rapids Inter-Tribal
Council
45 Lexington NW
Grand Rapids, MI 49504

Inter-Tribal Council of Michigan
405 E. Easterday Ave.
Sault Ste. Marie, MI 49783

Michigan Indian Benefit
Association
820 W. Saginaw St.
Lansing, MI 48915

Michigan Indian Child Welfare
120 Ridge St.
P. O. Box 537
Sault Ste. Marie, MI 49783

North American Indian
Association of Detroit
360 John Rd.
Detroit, MI 48226

Saginaw Inter-Tribal
Association
3239 Christy Way
Saginaw, MI 48603

Southeastern Michigan Indians
P. O. Box 861
Warren, MI 48090

MINNESOTA

American Indian Fellowship
2 E. 2nd St.
Duluth, MN 55802

URBAN INDIAN SERVICE PROJECTS

American Indian Health Care
Association
245 E 6th St., Suite 815
St. Paul, MN 55101

American Indian Movement
Peacemaker Center
2300 Cedar Ave. S.
Minneapolis, MN 55404

Indian Family Services
1305 E. 24th St.
Minneapolis, MN 55404

Minneapolis, Indian Center
1530 E. Franklin Ave.
Minneapolis, MN 55404

National Indian Education
Association
1115 2nd Ave. S.
Ivy Tower Bldg.
Minneapolis, MN 55403

Upper Midwest American
Indian Center
1113 W. Broadway
Minneapolis, MN 55411

United Church of Christ Council
of American Indian Ministry
22 W. Franklin Ave.
Minneapolis, MN 55404

St. Paul Indian Center
506 Kenny Rd.
St. Paul, MN 55101

MISSOURI
Heart of America Indian Center
1340 E. Admiral Blvd.
Kansas City, MO 64106

Southwest Missouri Indian
Center
322 E. Pershing, Suite A
Springfield, MO 65806

American Indian Center
4648 Gravios Blvd.
St. Louis, MO 63116

MONTANA
Anaconda Indian Alliance
P. O. Box 1108
524 E. Park
Anaconda, MT 58711

Billings American Indian
Council
P. O. Box 853
Billings, MT 59103

I.D.E.A., Inc.
P. O. Box 726
Miles City, MT 59301

Great Falls Indian Education
Center
P. O. Box 2531
Great Falls, MT 59403

Helena Indian Alliance
436 N. Jackson
Helena, MT 59601

Montana Inter-Tribal Policy
Board
2303 Grant Ave., Suite 5
Billings, MT 59102

Montana United Indian
Association
436 N. Last Chance Gulch #2
Helena, MT 59601

Missoula Qua-Qui Corporation
508 Toole Ave.
Missoula, MT 59801

Native American Center
P. O. Box 2612
Great Falls, MT 59403

North American Indian Alliance
P. O. Box 285
12 E. Galena
Butte, MT 59701

NEBRASKA
American Indian Center
613 S. 16th St.
Omaha, NE 68102

Lincoln Indian Center
1100 Military Rd.
Lincoln, NE 68508

Native American Public
Broadcasting Consortium
P. O. Box 83111
Lincoln, NE 68501

Nebraska Inter-Tribal
Development Corporation
Rte. 1, P. O. Box 66A
Winnebago, NE 68701

NEW MEXICO
All Indian Pueblo Council
P. O. Box 6507
Albuquerque, NM 87197

American Indian Law Center
University of New Mexico
P. O. Box 4456, Station A
Albuquerque, NM 87196

American Indian Nations
Region Save The Children
5101 Copper NE
Albuquerque, NM 87196

American Indian Scholarship
Fund
335 Jefferson St. SE., Suite D
Albuquerque, NM 87108

American Indian Tribal
Government and Policy
Consultants
1803 Carlisle NE
Albuquerque, NM 87110

Eight Northern Indian Pueblos
Council
P. O. Box 969
San Juan Pueblo, NM 87566

Farmington Inter-Tribal Council
P. O. Box 2322
Farmington, NM 87401

Five Dandoval Indian Pueblos
P. O. Box 580
Bernalillo, NM 87004

Indian Arts and Crafts
Association
4301 Lead SE
P. O. Box 40013
Albuquerque, NM 87102

Indian Pueblo Cultural Center
2401 12th St. NW
Albuquerque, NM 87102

Institute of American Indian
Arts College of Santa Fe
Alexis Hall St.
Michael's Drive
Santa Fe, NM 87501

URBAN INDIAN SERVICE PROJECTS

Inter-Tribal Indian Ceremonial Association
P. O. Box One
Church Rock, NM 87311

National Indian Council on Aging
P. O. Box 2088
Albuquerque, NM 87103

National Indian Youth Council
318 Elm St. SE
Albuquerque, NM 87102

New Mexico Indian Education Association
506 Lake St.
Albuquerque, NM 87105

Ramah Navajo School Board
CPO Drawer A
Pine Hill, NM 87321

Southwestern Association on Indian Affairs
P. O. Box 1964
Santa Fe, NM 87501

Ten Southern Pueblos Council
Governor, Pueblo of Acoma
P. O. Box 309
Acomita, NM 87034

NEW YORK
American Indian Community House
842 Broadway, 8th Floor
New York City, NY 10003

Association of American Indian Affairs
432 Park Ave. S.
New York City, NY 10016

Buffalo North American Indian Culture Center
1047 Grant St.
Buffalo, NY 14207

International Indian Treaty Council
777 UN Plaza, Room 10 F
New York City, NY 10017

Marquette League for Catholic Indian Missions
1011 1st Ave.
New York City, NY 10022

Museum of the American Indian Heye Foundation
Broadway at 155th St.
New York City, NY 10032

Native American Cultural Center
2115 E. Main ST.
Rochester, NY 14609

National Committee on Indian Worship of the Episcopal Church
815 Second Ave.
New York City, NY 10017

North American Indian Club of Syracuse and Vicinity
P. O. Box 851
Syracuse, NY 13201

NEVADA
Inter-Tribal Council of Nevada
650 S. Rock Blvd., Suite 11
Reno, NV 98502

Las Vegas Indian Center
418 Hoover Ave.
Las Vegas, NV 89101

Nevada Urban Indians
971 E. 6th St.
Reno, NV 89512

NORTH CAROLINA
Cumberland County Association of Indian People
102 Indian Drive
Fayetteville, NC 28301

Guilford Native Americans Association
P. O. Box 5623
Greensboro, NC 27403

Metrolina Native American Association
800 Briar Creek Rd., Suite CC-13
Charlotte, NC 28205

NORTH DAKOTA
Fargo-Moorhead Indian Center
P. O. Box 42
Fargo, ND 58107

OHIO
Native American Indian Center
1535 S. High St.
Columbus, OH 43207

Ohio Indian Center
3949 Dryden Dr.
North Olmsted, OH 44070

OKLAHOMA
Association of American Indian Physicians
6805 South Western, Suite 504
Oklahoma City, OK 73139

Cherokee National Historical Society
P. O. Box 515
Tahlequah, OK 74464

Creek Indian Memorial Association
Creek Council House Museum
Okmulgee, OK 74447

Daughters of the Trail of Tears
P. O. Box 580
Okmulgee, OK 74447

Indian Head Start Directors Association
107 Carol St.
Tahlequah, OK 74464

Indian Health Care Resource Center
P. O. Box 184
Tulsa, OK 74119

Inter-Tribal Council of Northeastern Oklahoma
P. O. Box 1308
Miami, OK 74354

Native American Center
2900 S. Harvey
Oklahoma City, OK 73109

Tulsa Native American Coalition
1740 W . St.
Tulsa, OK 74107

Viennese Era Veterans Inter-Tribal Association
Vet Center
4111 N. Lincoln Blvd.
Oklahoma City, OK 73105

URBAN INDIAN SERVICE PROJECTS

OREGON
Association of American Indian Research and Resource Institute
410 NW 18th St., #101
Portland, OR 97209

Columbia River Inter-Tribal Fisheries Commission
2705 E. Burnside, Suite 114
Portland, OR 97214

Native American Rehabilitation Association of the Northwest
3020 SE Hawthorne
Portland, OR 97214

Organization of the Forgotten American
3949 S. 6th St., #205
Klamath Falls, OR 97601

Oregon Indian Education Association
1053 Koala N.
Salem, OR 97303

Urban Indian Council
P. O. Box 3198
Portland, OR 97208

PENNSYLVANIA
American Friends Service Committee
1501 Cherry St.
Philadelphia, PA 19102

American Indian Research and Resource Institute
Gettysburg College
P. O. Box 576
Gettysburg, PA 17325

Council of Three Rivers
200 Charles St.
Pittsburg, PA 15238

United American Indian of the Delaware Valley
225 Chestnut St.
Philadelphia, PA 19106

RHODE ISLAND
Rhode Island Council
444 Friendship St.
Providence, RI 02907

SOUTH CAROLINA
South Carolina Council on Native Americans
P. O. Box 219221
Columbia, SC 29221

SOUTH DAKOTA
American Indian Culture Research Center
P. O. Box 98
Blue Cloud Abbey
Marvin, SD 57251

American Indian Service Center
100 W 6th St.
Sioux Falls, SD 57102

Institute of Indian Studies
University of South Dakota
Vermillion, SD 57069

Rapid City Indian Service Council
P. O. Box 7038
Rapid City, SD 57709

Women of All Red Nations
P. O. Box 2508
Rapid City, SD 57709

TENNESSEE
United South and Eastern Tribes
1101 Kermit Dr., Suite 800
Nashville, TN 37217

TEXAS
American Indian Center of Dallas
1314 Munger Blvd.
Dallas, TX 75206

Cultural Center for the American Indian
1269 N. Post Oak, #160
Houston, TX 77055

Dallas Inter-Tribal Center
209 E. Jefferson
Dallas, TX 75203

Society for American Indian Studies and Research
P. O. Box 443
Hurst, TX 76053

UTAH
Indian Center of Salt Lake
21 E. Kelsey
Salt Lake City, UT 84111

LDS Social Service Indian Student Placement Program
50 E. North Temple
Salt Lake City, UT 84150

Salt Lake Indian Health Center
508 E. South Temple, #219
Salt Lake City, UT 84102

Utah Navajo Development Council
P. O. Box 908
Blanding, UT 84511

VERMONT
Abanaki Self-Help
P. O. Box 276
Swanton, VT 05499

VIRGINIA
American Indian Bar Association
6017 Franconia Forest Lane
Alexandria, VA 22310

American Indian Heritage Foundation
6051 Arlington Blvd.
Falls Church, VA 22044

WASHINGTON
American Indian Community Center
N 1007 Columbus
Spokane, WA 99202

Central Washington Indian Association
106 S. 4th St.
Yakima, WA 98901

Kitsap County Indian Center
1200 Fairgrounds Rd.
Bremerton, WA 98310

National Coalition to Support Indian Treaties
814 NE 40th
Seattle, WA 98105

URBAN INDIAN SERVICE PROJECTS

Northwest Indian Fisheries
Commission
2625 Parkmont Lane SW,
Bldg. C
Olympia, WA 98502

Seattle Indian Health Board
1122 12th Ave. S.
P. O. Box 3364
Seattle, WA 98114

Seattle Indian Center
2220 Second Ave.
Seattle, WA 99205

United Indians of All Tribes
Foundation
C-99305 Discovery Pk.
Seattle, WA 98199

WISCONSIN

Great Lakes Inter-Tribal Council
P. O. Box 9
Lac de Flambeau, WI 54538

Milwaukee Indian Health Board
930 N 27th St.
Milwaukee, WI 53208

United Amerindian Health
Center
401 9th St.
Green Bay, WI 54304

DEMOGRAPHICS

INDIAN POPULATION 1990 CENSUS

STATE	INDIANS IN 1980	% OF '80 TOTAL	INDIANS IN 1990	% OF '90 TOTAL
ALABAMA	7,583	0.2	16,506	0.4
ALASKA			85,698	
ARIZONA	152,745	5.6	203,527	5.6
ARKANSAS	9,428	0.5	12,773	0.5
CALIFORNIA	201,369	0.9	242,164	0.8
COLORADO			27,776	
CONNECTICUT	4,533	0.1	6,654	0.2
DELAWARE	1,328	0.2	2,019	0.3
DISTRICT OF COLUMBIA	1,031	0.2	1,466	0.2
FLORIDA			36,335	
GEORGIA	7,616	0.1	13,348	0.2
HAWAII	2,768	0.3	5,099	0.5
IDAHO			13,780	
ILLINOIS	16,283	0.1	21,836	0.2
INDIANA	7,836	0.1	12,720	0.2
IOWA	5,455	0.2	7,349	0.3
KANSAS	15,373	0.7	21,965	0.9
KENTUCKY	3,610	0.1	5,769	0.2
LOUISIANA	12,065	0.3	18,541	0.4
MAINE			5,998	
MARYLAND	8,021	0.2	12,972	0.3
MASSACHUSETTS			12,241	
MICHIGAN	40,050	0.4	55,638	0.6
MINNESOTA	35,016	0.9	49,909	1.1
MISSISSIPPI	6,180	0.2	8,525	0.3
MISSOURI	12,321	0.3	19,835	0.4
MONTANA	37,270	4.7	47,679	6.0
NEBRASKA	9,195	0.6	12,410	0.8
NEVADA	13,308	1.7	19,637	1.6
NEW HAMPSHIRE	1,352	0.1	2,134	0.2
NEW JERSEY	8,394	0.1	14,970	0.2
NEW MEXICO			134,355	
NEW YORK	39,582	0.2	62,651	0.3
NORTH CAROLINA	64,652	1.1	80,155	1.2
NORTH DAKOTA	20,158	3.1	25,917	4.1
OHIO	12,239	0.1	20,358	0.2
OKLAHOMA	169,459	5.6	252,420	8.0
OREGON	27,314	1.0	38,496	1.4
PENNSYLVANIA	9,465	0.1	14,733	0.1
RHODE ISLAND	2,896	0.3	4,071	0.4
SOUTH CAROLINA			8,246	
SOUTH DAKOTA	44,968	6.5	50,573	7.3
TENNESSEE			10,039	
TEXAS	40,075	0.3	65,877	7.3
UTAH			24,283	
VERMONT	984	0.2	1,696	0.3
VIRGINIA	9,454	0.2	15,282	0.2
WASHINGTON			81,483	
WEST VIRGINIA			2,458	
WISCONSIN	29,499	0.6	39,387	0.8
WYOMING	7,094	1.5	9,479	2.1
TOTALS	**1,097,971**	**0.6**	**1,959,234**	**0.8**

BROADCAST

These radio and television stations devote a sizeable portion of air time to programs that are sensitive to American Indians. Production companies owned or staffed with American Indians are also listed.

ALABAMA
WASG-AM
1210 S. Main St.
Atmore, AL 36502
(205) 368-2511

ALASKA
ASRC Communications, Inc.
P. O. Box 129
Barrow, AK 99723
(907) 852-8633

KBRW-AM
P. O. Box 109
1695 Okpik St.
Barrow, AK 99723
(907) 852-6811

KYUK-AM & TV
P. O. Box 468
Bethel, AK 99559

KUAC Radio
Fairbanks, AK 99701
(907) 474-7491

KTOO-FM
224 4th St.
Juneau, AK 99801
(907) 586-1670

KRBD-FM & KTKN-AM
P. O. Box 6855
Ketchikan, AK 99901

KOTZ Radio
P. O. Box 78
Kotzebue, AK 99752
(907) 442-3434

National Native News
Alaska Public Radio Network
4640 Old Seward Highway, #202
Anchorage, AK 99503
(907) 563-7733

Metlakatla Indian Community Cable TV
P. O. Box 458
Metlakatla, AK 99926

ARIZONA
KNCC-FM
Navajo Community College
Tsaile, AZ 85445
(602) 724-3311

KNNB-FM
P. O. Box 310
Whiteriver, AZ 85941
(602) 338-4371

KTNN-AM
P. O. Box 2569
Window Rock, AZ 86515

KTVK-TV
3435 N. 16th St.
Phoenix, AZ 85016
(602) 263-3333

KUAT-AM
University of Arizona
Tucson, AZ 85721

Navajo Nation Office of Broadcast Services
P. O. Box 308
Window Rock, AZ 86515

CALIFORNIA
The American Indian Hour
P. O. Box 4187
Inglewood, CA 90309
(213) 299-1810

KIDE-FM
P. O. Box 1220
Hoopa, CA 95546
(916) 625-4245

KPOO-FM
P. O. Box 11008
San Francisco, CA 94101
(415) 346-5373

Round Valley Radio Project
P. O. Box 8
Covelo, CA 95428

COLORADO
KGNU
1900 Folsom St., #100
P.O. Box 865
Boulder, CO 80302
(303) 449-4885

KSUT-FM
P. O. Box 737
Ignacio, CO 81137
(303) 563-4507

MAINE
WMCM-FM/WRKD-AM
415 Main St.
Rockland, CO 48411

WQDY-AM/FM
281 Main St.
Calais, ME 04619

MINNESOTA
First Person Radio
Migizi Communications
3123 E. Lake St., Suite 200
Minneapolis, MN 55406
(612) 721-6631

KARE-TV
8811 Olson Memorial Highway
Golden Valley, MN 55427
(612) 546-1111

KTCA-TV/KTCI-TV
172 E. 4th St.
St. Paul, MN 55101
(612) 222-1717

BROADCAST

Red Lake Chippewa Radio
Project
Red Lake, MN 56671

MONTANA
Blackfeet Media
Blackfeet Tribe
P. O. Box 850
Browning, MT 59417
KBFT-FM
P. O. Box 819
Browning, MT 59417

KFBB-TV
P. O. Box 1139
Great Falls, MT 59403
(406) 453-4377
KOBL-TV
Dull Knife Memorial College
P. O. Box 206
Lame Deer, MT 59043

KZIN-FM/KSEN-AM
830 Oilfield Ave.
Shelby, MT 59425

NEBRASKA
KCSR-AM
Chardon, NE 69337
(308) 432-5545

Native American Public
Broadcasting Consortium
P.O. Box 83111
Lincoln, NE 68501

Omaha Cable TV Service
Omaha Indian Reservation
P. O. Box 368
Macy, NE 68039

NEW MEXICO
KNME-TV
1130 University Blvd. NE
Albuquerque, NM 87102

KOAT-TV
P. O. Box 25982
Albuquerque, NM 87125

KSHI-FM
P. O. Box 339
Zuni, NM 87327
(505)782-4811

KTDB-FM
P. O. Box 18
Ramah, NM 87121
(505) 783-5456

NEW YORK
Akwesasne Free Radio
C/O Ray Cook
Rooseveltown, NY 13683
CKON-FM
Mohawk Radio
P. O. Box 140
Rooseveltown, NY 13683

WBAI-FM
505 8th Ave.
New York, NY 10018
(212) 279-0707

NORTH CAROLINA
Eastern Band of Cherokee
Indian Cable TV Service
P. O. Box 455
Cherokee, NC 28719

WPSU-TV
Pembroke State University
Pembroke, NC 28372

NORTH DAKOTA
Fort Berthold Communications
P. O. Box 220
New Town, ND 58763

KEYA-FM
P. O. Box 190
Belcourt, ND 58316
(701) 477-5686

KMHA-FM
P. O. Box 220
New Town, ND 58763
(701) 627-3686

Standing Rock Cable
TV Service
Standing Rock Tribal Council
Fort Yates, ND 58538

OKLAHOMA
Kiowa Tribal Radio Station
P. O. Box 361
Carnegie, OK 73015
(405) 654-2300

KOTV-TV
302 S. Frankfort
Tulsa, OK 74107

OREGON
Confederated Tribes
Telecommunication Project
P. O. Box 584
Warm Springs, OR 97761

KPTV-TV
Indian Time
Portland, OR 97230

KWSI-FM
P. O. Box 489
Warm Springs, OR 97761

SOUTH DAKOTA
KILI-FM
Lakota Communications
P. O. Box 150
Porcupine, SD 57772
(605) 867-5002
KINI-FM
Rosebud Education Association
St. Francis, SD 57572
(605) 747-2291

KUSD-TV
310 E. Clark St.
Vermillion, SD 57069

UTAH
American Indian TV Services
Room 234-HRCB
Brigham Young University
Provo, UT 84602

WASHINGTON
KRNB-FM
P. O. Box 96
Neah Bay, WA 98357

Olympic TV Cable
P. O. Box 88
Port Orchard, WA 98366

Quinalt Indian Nation
P. O. Box 235
Taholah, WA 98587

WISCONSIN
WOJB-FM
Rte. 2, P. O. Box 2788
Hayward, WI 54843
(715) 634-2100

WIRC-FM
University of Wisconsin
216 College of Professional
Studies
Stevens Point, WI 54481
(715) 346-2746

WYOMING
KIEA-FM
Wind River Indian Education
Association
Wyoming Indian High School
Ethete, WY 82520
(307) 332-2793

PERIODICALS

This is by no means a complete listing of all American Indian publications.

ALASKA

Alaska Federation of Natives News
411 W. 4th Ave., Suite 301
Anchorage, AL 99501

Alaska Native Magazine
Alaska Native News, Inc.
P. O. Box 220230
Anchorage, AK 99522
(907)243-8730

Arctic Village Echoes
Arctic Village School
Arctic Village, AK 99722

Bering Straits Agluktuk
Bering Straits Native Corporation
P. O. Box 1008
Nome, AK 99762

Calistem Erini
Calista Corp.
601 W. 5th St., #200
Anchorage, AK 99501

Maneluk Report
P. O. Box 256
Kotzebue, AK 99752

Point Hope News
Point Hope Village
Point Hope, AK 99766

Sealaska Shareholder
Sealaska Corp.
One Sealaska Plaza, 400
Juneau, AK 99801

Spectrum Press
Anchorage Community College
2533 Providence Ave.
Anchorage, AK 99504

Theata
Cross Cultural Communications Dept.
University of Alaska
Alaskan Native Program
Fairbanks, AK 99708
(907) 474-7181

Tlingit/Haida Tribal News
Tlingit/Haida Central Council
One Sealaska Plaza, Suite 300
Juneau, AK 99801
(312) 784-1050

Tlin Tsim Hai
Ketchikan Indian Corp.
429 Deermont
Ketchikan, AK 99901

Tundra Drums
P. O. Box 468
Bethel, AK 99559

The Tundra Times
P. O. Box 104480
Anchorage, AK 99510-4480

Utkegvik Natchik
Barrow Junior High School
Barrow, AK 99723

The Voice of Brotherhood
423 Seward St.
Juneau, AK 99801

ARIZONA

American Indian Art Magazine
7314 E. Osborn Dr.
Scottsdale, AZ 85251
(602) 994-5445

Au-Authm Action News
Rte. 1, P. O. Box 216
Scottsdale, AZ 85251

Awattim Awahan
C/O Salt River Tribal Office
Rte. 1, P. O. Box 700
Scottsdale, AZ 85251

Bear Track
Phoenix College
1202 W. Thomas Rd.
Phoenix, AZ 85013

Bizhii
Cibecue Community School
Cibecue, AZ 85911
(602) 332-4480

Browning Sentinel
National Association of Blackfeet Indians
P. O. Box 340
Browning, MT 59417

Canyon Shadows
General Delivery
Supai, AZ 86435

Contemporary Indian Affairs
Navajo Community College
Tsaile, AZ 86556

Crowndancer
San Carlos Apache Tribe
P. O. Box 0
San Carlos, AZ 85550

Eagle Free Press
Phoenix Indian Center, Inc.
333 W. Indian School Rd.
Phoenix, AZ 85013
(602) 256-2000

PERIODICALS

Fort Apache Scout
P. O. Box 898
Whiteriver, AZ 85941

Gila River News
P. O. Box 97
Sacaton, AZ 85247

Gum-U
P. O. Box 168
Peach Springs, AZ 86425

Hopi Action News
Winslow Mail
Winslow, AZ 86047

Hopi Crier
Hopi Day School
Oraibi, AZ 86039

Indian Highways
Cook Christian Training School
708 S. Lindon Lane
Tempe, AZ 85281

Indian Programs
University of Arizona
Tucson, AZ 85721

Journal of American Indian Education
Center for Indian Education
Farmer Bldg. Room 415
Arizona State University
Tempe, AZ 85287
(602) 965-6292

Manataba Messenger
P. O. Box 810
Parker, AZ 85344

Native Peoples
Media Concepts Group, Inc.
1833 North Third St.
Phoenix, AZ 85004-1502

Navajoland Publications
Navajo Tribal Museum
Window Rock, AZ 86515

Navajo Times Today
Navajo Times CO,
P. O. Box 310
Window Rock, AZ 86515
(602) 871-5400

Papago Bulletin
P. O. Box 364
Sells, AZ 85634

Papago Runner
P. O. Box 837
Sells, AZ 85634

Pascua Pueblo News
4821 W. Calle Vicam
Tucson, AZ 85706

Pima-Maricopa Echo
Gila River Indian Community
P. O. Box 338
Sacaton, AZ 85247

Qua-Toqti
Hopi Publishers
P. O. Box 266
Kykotsmovi, AZ 86039
(602) 734-2425

Quechan News
Fort Yuma Indian Reservation
P. O. Box 1169
Yuma, AZ 85364

Red Earth News
37 E. Indian School Rd.
Phoenix, AZ 85012

Redskin
Phoenix Indian High School
Phoenix, AZ 85012

River Tribes Review
Colorado River Agency
Parker, AZ 85012

Rough Rock News
Dine'Biolta'Daahani
Rough Rock Demonstration
School, P. O. Box 217
Rough Rock, AZ 86503

Sandpainter
P. O. Box 791
Chinle, AZ 86503

Smoke Signals
Colorado River Indian Tribes
Rte. 1, P. O. Box 23-B
Parker, AZ 85344

Smoke Signals
National Council of Bureau of
Indian Affairs Educators
P. O. Box 5
Tuba City, AZ 86045
(602) 283-4211

Smoki Ceremonials And Snake Dance
Smoki People, P. O. Box 123
Prescott, AZ 86302
(602)778-5228

Sundevil Roundup
Rough Rock Community High School
Star Route 1
Rough Rock, AZ 85021

The Thunderer
American Indian Bible Institute
100020 N. 15th Ave.
Phoenix, AZ 85021

White Mountain Apache Newspaper
P. O. Box 700
White River, AZ 85941

White Mountain Eagle
P. O. Box 1570
Show Low, AZ 85901

Wi Guaba
Havasupai Tribal Council
P. O. Box 10
Supai, AZ 86435

Yaqui Bulletin
4730 W. Calle Tetakusin
Tucson, AZ 85910

CALIFORNIA

The American Indian
225 Valencia St.
San Francisco, CA 94103

American Indian Culture And Research Journal
American Indian Studies Center
Room 3220 Campbell Hall,
UCLA
405 Hilgard Ave.
Los Angeles, CA 90024

PERIODICALS

California Newsdrum
225 Valencia St.
San Francisco, CA 94103

Ech-Ka-Nav-Cha
500 Merrian
Needles, CA 92363

The Evanpaha
American Indian Lore
Association
P. O. Box 9698
Anaheim, CA 92802

Five Feathers News
Tribe of Five Feathers
P. O. Box W
Lompoc, CA 93436

Indian Archives
Antelope Indian Circle
P. O. Box 790
Susanville, CA 961130

The Indian Crusader
American Indian Liberation
Crusade, Inc.
4009 S. Halldale Ave.
Los Angeles, CA 90062
(213) 299-1810

Native Self-Sufficiency
Seventh Generation Fund for
Indian Development, Inc.
P. O. Box 10
Forestville, CA 95436
(707) 887-1559

Speaking Leaves
American Indian Cultural Group
P. O. Box 2000
Vacaville, CA 95688

Stealing of California
Native American Training
Association Institute
P. O. Box 1505
SACRAMENTO, CA 95807

Teepee Talk
P. O. Box 501
Portersville, CA 93258

Temipite Topics
P. O. Box 5396
Fresno, CA 93755

Tribal Spokesman
Inter-Tribal Council of California
1314 H St., #100
Sacramento, CA 95814

United Lumbee Nation Times
United Lumbee Nation of North
Carolina and America
P. O. Box 512
Fall River Mills, CA 96028
(916)336-6701

Whispering Winds
Tule River Tribal Council
Porterville, CA 93258

COLORADO

American Indian Review
National Urban Indian Council
10068 University Park Station
P. O. Box 10068
Denver, CO 80210
(303)698-2911

*Echo Towaoc Community
Newspaper*
Ute Mountain Tribe
Towaoc, CO 81334

*Oyate Nate Nata Yazadi
Phezuta*
University of Colorado
Boulder, CO 80309

Southwestern Lore
Colorado Archaeological
Society, Inc.
P. O. Box 36217
Denver, CO 80236
(303) 236-8675

Southern Ute Drum
P. O. Box 737
Tribal Affairs Bldg.
Ignacio, CO 81137

Winds of Change
American Indian Science and
Engineering Quarterly
1630 30th St., Suite 301
Boulder, CO 80301

CONNECTICUT

Artifacts
American Indian Archaeological
Institute
P. O. Box 260
Washington, CT 06793
(203) 868-0518

Eagle Wing Press, Inc.
P. O. Box 579 MO
Naugatuck, CT 06770
(203) 274-6058

DISTRICT OF COLUMBIA

Indian Courts
National American Indian Court
Judges
1000 Connecticut Ave. NW,
Suite 401
Washington, D. C. 20036
(202) 296-0685

Indian Education
National Indian Education
Association
1819 H St. NW., Suite 800
Washington, D. C. 20006

Indian Law Reporter
601 E St. SE
Washington, D. C. 20004

Red Alert
Americans for Indian
Opportunity
3508 Garfield St. NW
Washington, D. C. 20007
(202) 338-8801

FLORIDA

ALLIGATOR TIMES
Seminole Tribe
6073 Stirling Rd.
Hollywood, FL 33024

Miccosukee Everglades News
Miccosukee Tribe of Florida
P. O. Box 440021, Tamiami
Station
Miami, FL 33144

The Seminole Tribune
Seminole Tribe
6333 NW 30th St.
Hollywood, FL 33024
(305) 583-7112

PERIODICALS

IDAHO
Coeur D'Alene Council Fires
Coeur D'Alene Tribal Council
Plummer, ID 83851

Nee-Me-Poc-Tum-Tyne
Lapwai, ID 83540

Nez Perce Tribal Newspaper
P. O. Box 305
Lapwai, ID 85342

Sho-Ban News
Shoshone-Bannock Tribal Council
P. O. Box 900
Fort Hall, ID 83293
(208) 238-3887

ILLNOIS
American Indian Community Services Directory
NAES College Press
2838 W. Peterson
Chicago, IL 60659

The Warrior
American Indian Center
1630 W. Wilson
Chicago, IL 60640

INDIANA
Indian Progress
Associated Committee of Friends on Indian Affairs
124 E. Washington St.
Winchester, IN 47394
(317) 584-8276

IOWA
Indian Country
Sac & Fox Settlement
Tama, IA 52339

The Iowa Indian
Sioux City Public Library
6th & Jackson Sts.
Sioux City, IA 51105

KANSAS
Drumbeat
U. S. Penitentiary
Leavenworth, KS 66048

Indian Leader
Haskell Indian Junior College
P. O. Box H1305
Lawrence, KS 66044

Journal of the West
P. O. Box 1009, 1531 Yuma
Manhattan, KS 66502

Nish-NaBa
American Indian Culture Group
P. O. Box 2
Lansing, KS 66043

MAINE
Mawiw-Kilun
Tribal Governors, Inc.
Indian Township
Princeton, ME 04668

Nation Notes
6 River Rd.
Indian Island
Old Town, ME 04468

MARYLAND
Daybreak
Eagle Eye Communications Group
P. O. Box 98
Highland, MD 20777

MASSACHUSETTS
The Circle
Boston Indian Council
105 S. Huntington Ave.
Jamaica Plain, MA 02130

Mittark Wampanoag Indians
P. O. Box 1048
Mashpee, MA 02649

MICHIGAN
Great Lakes Pathfinder
460 Spruce St.
Sault Ste. Marie, MI 49783

The Michigan Indian
Baker Olen Bldg. W, Room 313
3423 N. Logan St.
Lansing, MI 48926

Nishawbe News
Organization of North American Indian Students
Northern Michigan University
140 University Center
Marquette, MI 49855

Turtle Talk
457 Brairwood SE
Grand Rapids, MI 49504

Wasso-Gee-Wad-Nee
Council—Marquette Branch Prison
P. O. Box 779
Marquette, MI 49855

Win-Awaenen-Nisitotung
Sault Ste. Marie Tribe of Chippewa Indians
2218 Shunk Rd.
Sault Ste. Marie, MI 49783
(906) 635-6050

MINNESOTA
Anishinabe Dee-Bah-Gee-Mo-win
White Earth Reservation Tribal Council
P. O. Box 418
White Earth, MN 56591

Anishinabe News
P. O. Box 55
Stillwater, MN 55082

The Circle Newspaper
Minneapolis Native American Center
1530 E. Franklin Ave.
Minneapolis, MN 55404
(612) 871-4749

Communicator
Migizi Communications, Inc.
3123 E. Lake St., Suite 200
Minneapolis, MN 55406
(612) 721-6631

De-Bah-Ji-Mon
P. O. Box 308
Cass Lake, MN 56633

Fond Du Lac Reservation News
105 University Dr.
Cloquet, MN 55720

PERIODICALS

Indian Voice
American Indian Folklore Group
P. O. Box 55
Stillwater, MN 55082

Ini-Mi-Kwa-Zoo-Minl
Minnesota Chippewa Tribe
P. O. Box 217
Cass Lake, MN 56623

Mille Lac News
Star Route
Onamia, MN 56395

Miskweewa Pinaywin
Lakes Publishing Co.
Detroit Lakes, MN 56501

Moccasin Telegraph
Community Action Program
Grand Portage, MN 55605

Nett Lake News
Nett Lake, MN 55772

Ni-Mi-Kwa-Zoo-Min
Minnesota Chippewa Tribe
P. O. Box 217
Cass Lake, MN 56633

Oshkabewis
Indian Studies Program
Bemidji State University
Bemidji, MN 56601

Red Lake News
Red Lake Reservation
Red Lake, MN 56671

Speaking of Ourselves Ni-Mi-Kwa-Zoo-Min
Minnesota Chippewa Tribe
P. O. Box 217
Cass Lake, MN 56633

The Times
P. O. Box 450
Farmington, MN 87401

White Earth Reservation News
P. O. Box 274
White Earth, MN 56591

MISSISSIPPI
Choctaw Community News
Mississippi Band of Choctaw Indians
Rte. 7, P. O. Box 21
Philadelphia, MS 39350
(601) 656-5251

MONTANA
Absaraka
Crow Indian Agency
Crow Agency, MT 59022

An Chi Mo Win
Rocky Boy's Reservation
Chippewa Cree Tribe
P. O. Box Elder, MT 59521

Arrow
St. Labre Indian School
Ashland, MT 59003

Atome-Northern Cheyenne News
P. O. Box 401
Lame Deer, MT 59043

Blackfeet Tribal News
Blackfeet Media
P. O. Box 850
Browning, MT 59417

Char-Koosta
Confederated Salish and Kostensi Tribes
P. O. Box 278
Pablo, MT 59855
(406) 675-2000

Crow News
Crow Tribal Government
Crow Agency, MT 59022

Eyapioaye
Assiniboine and Sioux Tribes
Poplar, MT 59255

Glacier Reporter
P. O. Box R
Browning, MT 59417

Hunter Quarterly
North American Indian Center
P. O. Box 7
Deer Lodge, MT 59722

Indian Signs
Blackfeet Tribal Business Center
Browning, MT 59417

The Morning Star People
St. Labre Indian School
Ashland, MT 59003

Northern Cheyenne News
P. O. Box 401
Lame Deer, MT 59043

Rocky Boy's Native Voice
Rocky Boy's Health Board
P. O. Box Elder, MT 59521

Rocky Boy's News
Rocky Boy's Rte.
P. O. Box Elder, MT 59521

The Sun Child
Missoula Qua Qui Corp.
401 E. Railroad
Missoula, MT 59801
(406) 721-4494

Tsistsistas Press
P. O. Box 8
Lame Deer, MT 59255

NEBRASKA
Honga
American Indian Center of Omaha
3610 Dodge St., #2098
Omaha, NE 68131

Winnebago Indian News
Winnebago Tribal Council
Winnebago, NE 68701

NEW JERSEY
Attan-Akamik
Rankikus Rd., P. O. Box 225
Rankokous, NJ 80873

NEW MEXICO
The Apache Scout
Mescalero Reservation
Mescalero, NM 88340

Broncos Monthly News
Sanostee Rural Station
Shiprock, NM 87420

PERIODICALS

Eight Northern Pueblos News
Rte. 1, P. O. Box 71
Santa Fe, NM 87528

Elder Voices
National Indian Council on Aging
P. O. Box 2088
Albuquerque, NM 87103

Four Directions
Kiva Club
1812 Las Lomas NE
Albuquerque, NM 87131

Indian Extension News
New Mexico State University
P. O. Box 3AP
Las Cruces, NM 88003

Indian Forerunner
Eight Northern Pueblos
P. O. Box 927
San Juan Pueblo, NM 87566

Jicarilla Chieftan
Jicarilla Apache Tribe
P. O. Box 507
Dulce, NM 87528
(505) 759-3242

National Indian Council on Aging Update Quarterly
P. O. Box 2088
Albuquerque, NM 87103

Native American Scholar
Bureau of Indian Affairs Higher Education Program
P. O. Box 1788
Albuquerque, NM 87103

Oueblo Horizon
Indian Pueblo Cultural Center, Inc.
2401 12th St. NW
Albuquerque, NM, NM 87102

Pueblo Times
1860 Don Pasqual Rd.
Los Lunas, NM 87031
(505) 865-4508

Red Times
P. O. Box 46
Laguna, NM 87026

The Singing Sands
Ramah Navajo High School
Ramah, NM 87351

Southwestern Association of Indian Affairs, Inc. Quarterly
Roswell Printing Co.,
110 N. Pennsylvania
Roswell, NM 88201

Spawning the Medicine River
Institute of American Indian Arts Museum
1369 Cerrillos Rd.
Santa Fe, NM 87501
(505) 988-6281

Tsa'aszi Magazine of Navajo Culture
Tsa'Aszi Graphics Center
Ramah Navajo School Board
CPO P. O. Box 12
Pine Hill, NM 87321

Zuni Carrier
Zuni Pueblo
Zuni, NM 87327

NEVADA

The Desert Breeze
P. O. Box 256
Nixon, NV 89424

Duck Valley Roundup
P. O. Box 219
Owynee, NV 89832

Elko Community News
Nevada Intertribal Council
806 Holman Way
Sparks, NV 89431

Native American Annual
Native American Publishing Co., Inc.
P. O. Box 6338, 760 Mays Blvd.
Incline Village, NV 89450

The Native Nevadan
Nevada Intertribal Council
Reno-Sparks Colony
98 Colony Rd.
Sparks, NV 89502
(702) 359-9449

Valley Round Up
Shoshone-Paiute Business Council
P. O. Box 219
Owyhee, NV 89832

NEW YORK

Akwekon Literary Journal
Akwesasne Notes
P. O. Box 223
Mohawk Nation
Hogansburg, NY 13655

Akwesasne Notes
P. O. Box 196
Mohawk Nation
Rooseveltown, NY 13683
(518) 358-9531

American Indian News
Thunderbird American Indian Dancers
215 W. 23rd St.
New York, NY 10011
(212)741-9221

Indian Affairs
Association of American Indian Affairs
95 Madison Ave.
New York, NY 10016
(212)689-8720

Indian Time
Akwesasne Notes
P. O. Box 196
Mohawk Station
Rooseveltown, NY 13683
(518) 358-9535

Man-Ah-Atn
American Indian Community House
404 Lafayette St.
New York, NY 10003

Northeast Indian Quarterly
Cornell University
400 Caldwell Hall
Ithaca, NY 14850
(602) 255-6587

O-He-Yoy-Noh
Seneca Nation of Indians
Museum Annex Bldg., Rte. 1
Allegany Indian Reservation
Salamanca, NY 14779

PERIODICALS

Tonawanda Indian News
P. O. Box 64, Bloomingdale Rd.
Akron, NY 14001

Turtle Quarterly
Native American Center for
Living Arts
25 Rainbow Mall
Niagara Falls, NY 14801

NORTH CAROLINA

The Carolina Indian Voice
P. O. Box 1075
Pembroke, NC 28372
(919)521-2826

Cherokee One Feather
Eastern Band of Cherokee
Indians
P. O. Box 501
Cherokee, NC 28719
(704) 497-5513

Cherokee Times
76 River Rd.
Cherokee, NC 28719

Indian Time
North Carolina Commission on
Indian Affairs
P. O. Box 2722
Raleigh, NC 27611

The Lumbee Outreach
Lumbee Regional Development
Association
P. O. Box 68
Pembroke, NC 28372

Qualla Reservation News
Cherokee Agency
Cherokee, NC 28719

NORTH DAKOTA

The Action News
P. O. Box 607
New Town, ND 58763

Dakota Student
University of North Dakota
P. O. Box 8177, University
Station
Grand Forks, ND 58201

E'yanapaha
Devil's Lake Sioux Tribe
Public Information Office
Fort Totten, ND 58335

Standing Rock Star
P. O. Box 483
Fort Yates, ND 58538

Wahpeton Highlights
Wahpeton Indian School
Wahpeton, ND 58075

OKLAHOMA

American Indian Journal
Institute for the Development of
Indian Law
Oklahoma City University
School of Law
2501 N. Black welder
Oklahoma City, OK 73106
(405) 531-5337

American Indian Law Review
University of Oklahoma
College of Law
300 Timberdell Rd.
Norman, OK 73019
(405) 325-2840

Atoka Indian Citizen
P. O. Box 160
Atoka, OK 74525

Smoke Signals
Bacone College
Muskogee, OK 74401

Bishinik
Choctaw Nation
P. O. Drawer 1210
Durant, OK 74701

The Buckskin
Rte. 3
Eaufaula, OK 74701

Cavo Transporter
Cheyenne-Arapaho Veterans
Organization
P. O. Box 34
Concho, OK 73022

Cherokee Advocate
Cherokee Nation of Oklahoma
P. O. Box 948
Tahlequah, OK 74465

The Chickasaw Times
Chickasaw Nation Tribal
Government
P. O. Box 1548
Ada, OK 74820
(405) 436-2503

Coktv Tvleme
Seminole Nation of Oklahoma
P. O. Box 745
Wewoka, OK 74884

Comanche
Comanche Tribe of Oklahoma
P. O. Box 908
Lawton, OK 73502

Creek Nation News
Creek Nation of Oklahoma
Okmulgee, OK 74447

Five Tribes Journal
Five Civilized Tribes Foundation
Chickasaw Nation
P. O. Box 1548
Ada, OK 74820

Great Plains Journal
Institute of the Great Plains
Museum of the Great Plains
P. O. Box 68, 601 Ferris
Elmer Thomas Park
Lawton, OK 73502
(405) 353-5675

Hello Choctaw
P. O. Box 59
Durant, OK 74701

The Indian Journal
Indian Journal Printing Co.
Eufaula, OK 74432

Kiowa Indian News
P. O. Box 361
Carnegie, OK 73015

Muscogee Nation News
Muscogee (Creek) Nation
P. O. Box 580
Okmulgee, OK 74447
(918) 756-8700

Osage Nation News
P. O. Box 1346
Pawhuska, OK 74056

PERIODICALS

Sac and Fox News
Rte. 2, P. O. Box 246
Stroud, OK 74079

Screaming Eagle
2400 Southeast Circle Dr.
Bartlesville, OK 74006

Smoke Dreams
Riverside High School
Anadarko, OK 73005

Will Rogers Times
Will Rogers Memorial
P. O. Box 157
Claremore, OK 74018
(918) 341-0719

OREGON
Klamath Tribune
Klamath Tribe
P. O. Box 436
Chiloquin, OR 97624

Indian News
United Indian Women
5352 SE 89th St.
Portland, OR 97266

Lakota Oyate-Ko
Oregon State Penitentiary
2605 State St.
Salem, OR 97310

Mukluks Hemcunga
Organization of the Forgotten American
P. O. Box 1257
Klamath Falls, Or 97601

Native News
Indian Education Program
School District 463
200 N. Monroe
Eugene, OR 97402
(503) 687-3489

Smoke Signals
Confederated Tribes of the Grande Ronde Indian Community
P. O. Box 94
Grand Ronde, OR 97347
(503) 879-5253

Tomahawk
Oregon State University
P. O. Box 428
Warm Springs, OR 97761

PENNSYLVANIA
Hoina
P. O. Box 302
Leola, PA 17540

RHODE ISLAND
Cooper Beech Press
P. O. Box 1852
Providence, RI 02912

The Corn Planter
Rhode Island Indian Council
444 Friendship St.
Providence, RI 02907

SOUTH DAKOTA
Blue Cloud Quarterly
Blue Cloud Agency
P. O. Box 98
Marvin, SD 57251

Cheyenne River Agency News Bulletin
Eagle Butte, SD 57625

The Drumbeat
Crow Creek Reservation High School
Stephan, SD 57346

Eagle Butte News
Eagle Butte, SD 57625

Flandreau Spirit
Flandreau Indian High School
Flandreau, SD 57028

Great Plains Observer
218 South Egan
Madison, SD 57042

Keyapi News
P. O. Box 200
Fort Thompson, SD 57339

The Lakota Times
Native American Publishing
1920 Lombardy Dr.
Rapid City, SD 57701
(605) 341-0011

Little Sioux
Rosebud Education Society
St. Francis, SD 57572

Oglala Nation News
P. O. Box 320
Pine Ridge, SD 57770

Paha Sapa Wahose
c/o Student Special Services
Black Hills State College
Spearfish, SD 57783

Pierre Chieftan
Pierre Indian School
Pierre, SD 57783

Pierre Indian Learning Center News
Star Route 3
Pierre, SD 57501

Red Cloud Country
Red Cloud Indian School
Pine Ridge, SD 57770
(605) 867-5491

The Scout
Episcopal Church
Lower Brule, SD 57548

Sioux S'An Sun
PHS Indian Hospital
Sisseton, SD 57262

Sota-Eye-Ye-Yapi
P. O. Box 509
Agency Village, SD 57262

Todd County Tribune and Eyapah
Mission, SD 57555

Wanbli Ho: A Literary Arts Journal
Lakota Studies Creative Writing Program
Sinte Gleska College, P. O. Box 8
Mission, SD 57555

War Cry
P. O. Box 200
Fort Thompson, SD 57339

Wopeedam
Immaculate Conception Mission
Stephan. SD 57346

TENNESSEE
Indian Reader
806 E. Brooks Rd.
Memphis, TN 38116

PERIODICALS

The Uset Calumet
1101 Kermit Dr., Suite 800
Nashville, TN 37212

TEXAS
Four Winds
Hundred Arrows Press
P. O. Box 156
Austin, TX 78767
(512) 472-8877

Indian American Quarterly
P. O. Box 443
Hurst, TX 76053

Red Men Magazine
Great Council of U. S. Improved Order of Red Men
P. O. Box 683
Waco, TX 76703
(817) 756-1221

UTAH
Eagle's Eye
Brigham Young University
Office of Student Affairs
4th Floor ELWC
Provo, UT 84602
(801) 378-6263

Indian Affairs News
Brigham Young University
Provo, UT 84601

The Medicine Bag
SLC Indian Health Center
509 E. South Temple, #219
Salt Lake City, UT 84102
(801) 532-2034

St. Christopher's Mission
News Center
Bluff, UT 84512

Utah Indian Journal
Division of Indian Affairs
University of Utah
Salt Lake City, UT 84112

Ute Bulletin
Ute Indian Tribe
P. O. Box 220
Fort Duchesne, UT 84026

WASHINGTON
Buckskin Reporter
919 Larson Bldg.
6 South 2nd St.
Yakima, WA 98901

Chinook
215 Viking Union
Western Washington College
Bellingham, WA 98225

Confederated Indian Tribes
Washington State Penitentiary
P. O. Box 520
Walla Walla Washington 99362

Dsuq'Wub'Siatsub
Suquamish Tribe
P. O. Box 556
Suquamish, WA 98392

Dxwhida
National Coalition to Support Indian Treaties
814 NE 40th St.
Seattle, WA 98105
Indians Of All Tribes Club
P. O. Box 777
Monroe, WA 98272

Indian Notes
P. O. Box 66
Wellpinit, WA 99040

Indian Voice
P. O. Box 578
Sumner, WA 98390

Kee-Yoka
Swinomish Tribal Council
P. O. Box 338
La Connor, WA 98257

Klaah'Che'Min
Squaxin Tribal Center
Rte. 1, P. O. Box 257
Shelton, WA 98584

Lummi Squol Quol
2616 Kwina Rd.
Bellingham, WA 98226
(206) 734-8180

Makah Dakah
P. O. Box 547
Neah Bay, WA 98357

Makah Viewers
P. O. Box 115
Neah Bay, WA 98357

Many Smokes Metis/Earth Awareness Magazine
Bear Tribe Medicine Society
P. O. Box 9167
Spokane, WA 99206

Nan Itch Tenas
Indian Education Program
P. O. Box 1367
Tacoma, WA 98401

Native Northwest
P. O. Box 356
Toppenish, WA 98948

Northwest Indian Times
Gonzaga University
Spokane, WA 99202

Nugguam
Quinault Tribal Affairs
P. O. Box 1118
Taholah, WA 98587

The Renegade : A Strategy Journal of Indian Opinion
Survival of American Indian Associations
7803-A Samurai Dr. SE
Olympia, WA 98503
(206) 459-2679

See Yahtsub
6700 Totem Beach Rd.
Maryville, WA 98270

Smoke Talk
Brotherhood of American Indian
P. O. Box 500
Steilacoom, WA 98388

The Squaw's Message
Sisterhood of American Indian
P. O. Box 17
Big Harbor, WA 98335

Ti Swanni Itst
Skokomish Indian Tribal Center
Rte. 5, P. O. Box 432
Shelton, WA 98584

PERIODICALS

Tribal Tribune
Colville Tribe
P. O. Box 150
Nepelem, WA 99155

Yakima Drumbeat
Freindship House
P. O. Box 31
Toppenish, WA 98948

Yakima Nation Review
Yakima Indian Nation
P. O. Box 386
Toppenish, WA 98948
(509) 865-5121

WISCONSIN

Anishinaabe News
648 Holton Hall
University of Wisconsin
Milwaukee, WI 53201

Great Lakes Agency News
Great Lakes Indian Agency
Ashland, WI 54806

Great Lakes Indian News Bureau
Rte. 5, P. O. Box 5355
Hayward, WI 54843

The Ho Chunk
P. O. Box 311
Tomah, WI 54660

Kalihui Saks
P. O. Box 365
Oneida, WI 54155

Lac Courte Oreilles Journal
LCO Graphic Arts
Rte. 2
Hayward, WI 54843

Lac Du Flambeau Update
LDF Tribal Office
P. O. Box 67
Lac du Flambeau, WI 54538

Menominee Tribal News
P. O. Box 397
Keshena, WI 54135
(715) 799-3341

Native American Council
204 Hagestad Student Center
University of Wisconsin
River Falls, WI 54022

News from Indian Country
Rt. 2 P.O. Box 2900-A
Hayward, WI 54843

Red Cliff Tribal News
P. O. Box 529
Bayfield, WI 54814

Smoke Signals
Rte. 2, P. O. Box 400
Odanah, WI 54806

We Sa Mi Dong
Rte. 5, P. O. Box 5320
Hayward, WI 54843

WYOMING

American Indian News
Office of Native American Programs
P. O. Box 217
Fort Washakie, WY 82514

Arapahoe Agency Courier
Arapahoe Agency, WY 82510

Wind River Journal
Shoshone Tribe
P. O. Box 157
Fort Washakie, WY 82514

Wind River Rendezvous
St. Stephan's Mission
St. Stephan, WY 82524

GLOSSARY

Stereotypes are poor dyes which fade in the light of understanding.

aboriginal - native; belonging or pertaining to the original inhabitants of a region.

agency - an administrative government division empowered to act for another, e. g., a federal institution which dispenses services to Indians.

AIM - the American Indian Movement, a controversial militant organization founded in Minnesota in 1968, dedicated to promoting civil rights for Indians in Canada and the United States. Its objectives include exposing treaty violations and reformation of the Bureau of Indian Affairs. In protest, members briefly took over the Washington D. C. office of the Bureau of Indian Affairs in 1972, and have since illegally occupied several Indian historical sites and battlegrounds.

alcoholism - an illness caused by physical and psychological dependence on alcohol. Short-term effects include deterioration in personal standards and habits, mood changes, and memory loss. Alcoholism continues to be a serious problem for many Indians, although alcohol-related deaths among Indians were halved in the years 1975 to 1987 due to counselling and outreach programs. Injustice, poverty, lack of education, low self-esteem, and inadequate therapy are often cited as contributors to the problem. The availability of liquor is a tribal decision; about 55 reservations are wet, the rest are dry.

allotment - under the Dawes Act of 1887, the allocation of 160 acres to every Indian man in an unsuccessful attempt to undermine the Indian concept of communal land ownership and break up the reservation system.

alphabet Indian - "A to Z" books for children have often illustrated the letter "I" as "I is for Indian". Often the other letters are illustrated with objects. Indians, however, are not objects, and the editors of these books have somehow avoided choices such as "I is for Italian", or "J is for Jew."

American Indian - a diverse group of peoples in North, South, Central America and the Caribbean, whose ancestors most likely migrated from Asia through Alaska between 10,000 and 20,000 years ago. At the time of early European contact their cultures ranged from hunter-gatherers to elaborate civilizations with advanced mathematics and extensive libraries. They refer to themselves not as American Indians but as members of hundreds of individual nations, speaking distinct languages and maintaining diverse cultural and spiritual traditions. They live in varying degrees of autonomy, having generally been subjugated by more recent economically and politically dominant European immigrants. Although criteria vary by tribe and government agency, legal inclusion on tribal roles usually requires an individual to be one-quarter Indian by birth. As of 1990, people claiming American Indian heritage in the United States census numbered about 1.5 million; 800,000 live on or near reservations.

American Indian Religious Freedom Act (1978) - was a new federal policy to protect traditional Indian religious practices threatened by federal actions. In the United States, all Indian religious practices were outlawed by the Bureau of Indian Affairs until 1934. Freedom of religion was part of the 1968 Indian Civil Rights Act except the establishment clause limitations of the First Amendment which were not made applicable to tribal governments.

GLOSSARY

assimilation - a United States government policy of absorbing Indians into mainstream culture by incentive or coercion. Also called "acculturation" or "Americanization."

band - a subdivision of an Indian tribe, often made up of an extended family. Bands often adopt a sacred emblem identifying spiritual closeness with a specific animal.

BIA (Bureau of Indian Affairs) - Established in 1832 as part of the War Department to direct the relocation of Indians from their native lands to reservations, the Bureau of Indian Affairs was transferred to the United States Department of the Interior in 1849. Today, it oversees Indian reservations, directing many aspects of Indian economic and political life, usually maintaining authority over tribal governments. Often criticized for paternalism and heavy-handedness, the BIA has been the target of numerous investigations for impropriety, a 1989 United States Senate committee citing continuing "fraud, mismanagement and corruption" and tagging the agency as "a stifling bureaucratic presence."

boarding schools (Indian) - schools typically operated by missionaries or government employees in the United States and Canada in which Indian children were isolated from their families, often suffering brutal discipline in an effort to force their assimilate into the dominant European society. More than 500,000 Indian children attended these schools from the end of the last century until the 1960's.

buck - (slang) a racially-charged and disparaging term for an American Indian man.

chief - a European term accepted as a general reference to the often hereditary leader of a tribe or clan. For the most part, a chief's authority varied by tribe; historically leadership decisions have been subject to concensus or a council's approval. The term may be considered offensive if used to address any Indian other than the actual title-bearer.

cigar store Indian - originally a wooden statue of an American Indian wearing a parody of traditional dress, displayed at the entrance of a tobacco store. Also a derogatory term for assimilated Indians.

clan - a social group within a tribe, made up of several families who trace descent from a common ancestor and may share property. Marriage within the clan may be strictly prohibited.

constitutions - some American Indian tribes had constitutional forms of government. For example, the Iroquois Oral Constitution—the Great Law of Peace—preceded that of the United States by centuries, and was cited by Benjamin Franklin (Albany Congress, 1754) as an example set "by ignorant savages" for a successful union. The Cherokee constitution instituted self-government by elective democratic process. After the Indian Reorganization Act of 1934, many tribes adopted constitutions, subject to the approval of the Bureau of Indian Affairs.

coup - in traditional Indian warfare, touching an enemy with the hand or an object in the course of battle as a proof of bravery and an act of humiliation. Plains Indians "counted coup", sometimes with "coup sticks" rather than true weapons.

culture - the sum total of ways of living built up by a group of human beings and transmitted from one generation to another. Socially taught activities.

dancing - many tribes maintain unique, individual traditions of dancing, usually accompanied by drumming and singing. Some dances affirm a tribe's place in the cosmos, realigning harmony between the natural and spiritual elements of the universe. Others are entertaining or instructional in their dramatic content. Dances are often displayed during powwows, when prizes may be awarded for both dancing and costuming. Most public dances are traditional (social) dances; few religious (ceremonial) dances are open to the non-Indian public.

Dawes Act (General Allotment Act) (1887) - United States law that prepared Indians for eventual termination of the reservation system by granting 160-acre allotments to each male Indian, promoting private farming with the intention of easing assimilation. Surplus l

GLOSSARY

and was purchased inexpensively by the United States government and turned over to white settlers, often resulting in awkward checkerboarding of Indian and White ownership inside reservation boundaries. Teddy Roosevelt called it "a mighty pulverizing engine to break up the tribal mass." The act was a failure, primarily because of the American Indian concept of land not as a possession but rather as a spiritual and physical domain shared with all creatures, and reluctance to abandon their traditions. In a few decades, native people lost more than 90 million acres through misunderstanding, naivete, hardship, tax laws and swindles. The 1934 Indian Reorganization Act ended the allotment policy.

eagle feather - a religious object for many American Indians. The wearing of feathers often symbolizes honor or status. Eagles are not killed to acquire the feathers. Possession is regulated by modern law.

Economic Opportunity Act (1965) - law allowing Indian tribes and organizations to receive direct funding for their own initiatives in addressing social, educational, and economic needs, bypassing the sometimes burdensome bureaucracy of the Bureau of Indian Affairs.

enrolled - to be legally considered an Indian, an individual must be enrolled as a member of one of the federally recognized tribes. Government agencies and individual tribes often each have different criteria to determine who is an Indian.

Eskimo - a people inhabiting the Arctic areas of North America and Greenland. Traditionally, they have no overall sense of shared identity, but live and travel in small bands, hunting and fishing. They refer to themselves as Inuit, and although they now virtually all live in settled communities with varying degrees of reliance on the dominant Western economy, many maintain spiritual and totemic connections to the natural world through dance, ritual, storytelling, and song.

ethnicity - the distinctive social, cultural, linguistic, and physical attributes of a particular group.

ethnocentrism - the belief that aspects of one's own culture are superior to those of others. Christian proselytizing and assimilation are both examples of ethnocentrism.

federal recognition - legal recognition of a people as a tribe, making them eligible for federal services. There are many "unrecognized" tribes.

Five Civilized Tribes - shortly after contact with European immigrants, the Cherokee, Creek, Chickasaw, Choctaw and Seminole of the southern United States appeared to easily adopt many European manners and skills, probably because their traditional practices were already culturally advanced by European standards. E.g. the Cherokee had a written language and so easily formed the first tribal newspaper. Nonetheless, all five tribes were relocated to Indian Territory.

giveaway - a part of many American Indian events during which goods are, literally, given away out of charitable concern or to demonstrate the largesse of the host. Gift-giving is a long-standing tradition of Indian culture, which is less concerned with property than some.

going back to the blanket - a phrase used in disdain for Indians, including children, who reject assimilation.

happy hunting ground - a simplistic and often offensive reference to American Indians' concepts of the afterlife.

heathen or pagan - anyone considered irreligious, uncivilized, unenlightened, or unconverted to Judaism, Islam, or Christianity. Such references to Indians were usually based in ethnocentrism or naivete about the depth of Indian spirituality. Indians were often times referred to as heathens by racists, those who misunderstood their ways, or those who pursued an agenda of assimilation.

Indian Center - (or Friendship Center) a non-profit organization, often in an urban setting, that provides various social, cultural, educational, employment and health services for Indians.

Indian Citizenship Act (1924) - congression-

76

GLOSSARY

al act granting voting rights and citizenship in the United States to American Indians, motivated partly by acknowledgment of the service record of Indians in World War I. Indians were still considered outside the protection of the Bill of Rights, however.

Indian Civil Rights Act (1968) - act of Congress for the first time extending the protection of the Bill of Rights to Indians. Religious freedom, however, was not to be legislated until 1978.

Indian Claims Commission (1946) - act of Congress created to hear and rule on claims brought by Indians against the United States for unfulfilled treaty terms. It was terminated by Congress in 1978.

Indian country - (slang) any place populated primarily by American Indians.

Indian Education Act (1972) - gave Indians more direct access to funds for school programs.

Indian name - many Indians have been given names from their native languages as an expression of pride in their cultural heritage. Names are often given in "naming ceremonies," which for some tribes are elaborate occasions.

Indian nations - the unique and complex legal status of American Indians, as well as a self-concept Indian peoples hold as citizens of distinct tribal groups with specific and unique cultural and political identities.

Indian Removal Act (1830) - initiated the systematic, forced relocation of tribes in the east to "Indian Territory" west of the Mississippi in an effort to prevent altercations with arriving European settlers.

Indian Reorganization Act (Wheeler-Howard Act) (1934) - sometimes known as the "Indian New Deal," replaced the Dawes Act, providing for political and economic development of reservations, and the creation of autonomous tribal governments, all under increased Bureau of Indian Affairs supervision.

Indian Territory - an area comprising most of what is now Oklahoma, set aside in the early 1800's for Indian relocation by the United States government under the Indian Removal Act. Among the first to be relocated were the Five Civilized Tribes.

Iroquois League (League of Five Nations) - a powerful military alliance of eastern Indian tribes formed in the late sixteenth century. Governed by a Great Council, it comprised the Mohawks, Oneidas, Onondagas, Cayugas and Senecas, and, after 1710, the Tuscaroras.

legal status - most American Indians became voting United States Citizens in 1924 (Indian Citizenship Act), but remained outside the full protection of the federal Constitution. The Bill of Rights was not extended to Indians until 1968 (PL 90-284, Indian Civil Rights Act), and religious freedom was not legislated until 1978. Tribal members have additional, unique rights guaranteed by treaty and federal law. Indians pay local, state and federal taxes, including income taxes.

Little Bighorn, Battle of (June 25, 1876) - during a major military offensive against the allied Lakota, Dakota, Nakota, Arapaho and Cheyenne nations in South Dakota, General George Custer led a Seventh Cavalry force of over 200 men. Outnumbered 10 - 1, they were routed by an allied force of several Indian tribes who had been resisting incursions by white settlers into lands granted to them by treaty in 1868. Still, they were driven from the area shortly after the battle. Also called "Custer's Last Stand," it was the last major Indian victory over United States government forces.

medicine - the holistic concept of fostering harmony between the spiritual world and the natural world, or the objects or substances that represent efforts to achieve or recognize that harmony, such as medicine bundles.

medicine man - one who maintains tribal lore and rituals and interprets and attempts to control the supernatural. He or she applies powers to evoke visions, cure the sick, and to bring success, often by realigning the harmonies of the spiritual and the natural worlds. Medicine men are often highly respected members of their communities.

GLOSSARY

moccasin telegraph - phrase referring to the unofficial channels through which news may spread rapidly in Indian country. Similar to "grapevine."

National Congress of American Indians - formed in 1944, the country's oldest Indian advocacy organization, comprising more that 200 tribes.

noble savage - originally a European literary term referring to the romantic notion that, left alone, primitive man was superior to Europeans.

papoose - the Algonquin word for "baby", often mistakenly used to refer to any Indian infant.

paternalism - the practice of managing or governing a group in the manner of a father dealing with his children; often used to characterize the attitude toward Indians by the United States government, particularly the Bureau of Indian Affairs.

pidgin English - A language of convenience, usually developed for trade, combining elements of two or more languages. A fictitious and degrading version of pidgin English ("How", "Ugh!", "Heap big", "Me likum.") has been spoken by American Indian characters in comics, cartoons, and Western movies, making them appear homogeneous, inept, and stupid. Tonto is a notable example. In reality, Indians have no specific difficulty speaking English.

pipe (calumet) - Indian pipes were used to smoke various plant substances, such as tobacco or inner tree bark. They usually have a carved pipestone (catlinite) bowl and a long wooden stem decorated with porcupine quills, beads or feathers. Sacred pipes may be used only on special ceremonial occasions, while less spiritually significant "social pipes" may be smoked more regularly. Although a pipe was occasionally shared as a gesture of friendship, the concept of a "peace pipe" was an invention of European writers.

potlatch - a Northwest Coast tribal ceremony of feasting, speech making, singing and dancing in which an individual gives away or destroys his property to demonstrate his wealth and affirm a higher rank in the tribal hierarchy. The potlatch was banned by the Canadian government from 1884 to 1951.

powwow - a council, festival or reunion among Indians for feasting, socializing, trading and dancing. Originating among the Plains tribes, the celebration has spread to most of the other nations and remains a widespread, year-around feature of American Indian culture. Non-Indians are often invited.

prestige society - an Indian military, religious, or medicinal status group. Membership is based on skills, talents, or spirit-power.

Public Law 280 (1953) - enacted in the termination era to allow transfer of control of Indian lands from the federal government to individual states, thereby granting some states jurisdiction over reservations within their boundaries. Criticized for vagueness, it was used by some states to illegally exploit Indian lands. The Indian Civil Rights Act of 1968 was passed partially to address its shortcomings.

race - a group of people related by common descent, blood or heredity; any geographical, tribal, or national ethnic grouping.

racism - a doctrine supposing racial superiority or inferiority, or promoting racial persecution or domination.

redskin - a pejorative and highly offensive term for American Indian.

religion - Indian ritual establishes favorable relations with spiritual forces of the earth, the sea and the animal world. The Lakotas say mitakuye oyasin, meaning "all my relations," i. e., all elements of the world are intimately related. Indian religions generally do not distinguish between the sacred and the secular: everything is sacred. Some Indian religions today incorporate Christianity as a pantheistic aspect, while others are still firmly traditional, but most still hold a respect for others beliefs as a basic tenet. Most believe in a single great force or spirit. The last decade has seen an active renewal of interest in traditional religions.

GLOSSARY

relocation - the forced removal of tribes from one location to another, a common United States governmental practice in the 1800's. Beginning in the early 1950's, the federal government adopted a modern relocation policy, pressuring Indians to move from reservations to urban areas.

renegade - a person who deserts a cause, faith or party for another. Implies that the person originally freely agreed to the cause. Indians so termed had repudiated the United States government, or had concluded that cooperation was not in the best interest of their people. Often a derogatory term for any Indian who is perceived as uncooperative or overly independent.

rez - (slang) reservation.

reservation (known as "reserve" in Canada) - land set aside by federal or state governments for Indians. Originally, Indians were not allowed to leave. Most reservations have diminished to a fraction of their original size as land was sold or usurped by the government. Today, reservations are tribally held lands, protected by the United States government, and Indians are free to come and go. Economic conditions on reservations are typically poor, however some tribes have in recent decades been successful in establishing self-owned and managed businesses. There are more than 500 reservations in the United States, where about half of the country's Indian population resides.

scalping - a practice promoted by the leaders of the early American colonies, who paid bounties for Indian scalps. Some tribes also took enemies' scalps as trophies of victory. The practice was not as universal as it appeared in popular fiction. Some Indians believed that a person could not go to the afterlife if body parts were removed.

scout - an Indian who rode ahead to watch for trouble, or, an Indian hired by whites to track or gather information. Scouts sometimes assisted the United States government in subjugating Indians of other, enemy tribes.

self-determination - a major modern tribal and federal policy calling for Indian self-government and cultural renewal, set out in Indian Self-Determination and Educational Assistance Act (1974). The Act, intended to give tribes more influence over finances and educational programs, has been hampered by budgetary restrictions, factionalism, and red tape.

shaman - a term originally applied to traditional healers in northeast Asia for a traditional practitioner able to influence beneficial and malevolent spiritual entities.

sign language - although originally interpreted by Europeans as evidence of a lack of sophistication in the development of Indian languages, sign language actually supplemented sophisticated spoken communication, facilitating conversation between culturally diverse Plains tribes who often spoke mutually incomprehensible languages.

Song of Hiawatha - a purple poem (1855) by Henry Wadsworth Longfellow. Its repetition in American classrooms helped to inculcate many Indian stereotypes. Hiawatha has since become a disparaging term for an Indian woman.

sovereignty - the concept that Indian nations should maintain autonomous control over their own economic and political destinies. Some proponents argue that Indian nations should be treated as distinct political entities, able to independently negotiate with the United States State Department and foreign governments.

squaw - an American Indian woman, especially a wife. Frequently disparaging and usually offensive, it implies a form of chattel. In reality, women have a strong voice in many Indian communities.

stereotypes - trite, uninformed, often banal images or mocking characterizations implying that all members of a group or race are alike. Stereotypes replace observation and thought with bias and patterned response. The beliefs and lifestyles of millions of individuals, hundreds of tribes, cannot responsibly be reduced to a few simple equations. Indians today are often stereotyped as all poor, dirty, lazy, drunk, living on welfare.

GLOSSARY

Sun Dance - An annual Plains renewal rite to realign the relationship of man with spiritual forces. The Crow performed these ceremonies to avenge the killing of friends or relatives in battle. The most dramatic rituals involved self-torture by warriors, resulting in spiritual visions. Outlawed, the Sun-Dance has seen some revival in recent decades. It is one of the few religious ceremonies generally open to the public.

sweathouse - a structure in which men expose themselves to extreme heat from a fire or by throwing water on hot stones, in an act of ritual spiritual purification through perspiring. Large sweathouses are sometimes called "sweatlodges".

termination - a policy of the federal government begun under President Eisenhower in 1953, intended to cut costs by ending the special protective relationship between the United States government and Indian tribes, and promote the demise of Indian tribal and communal organization. Some tribes were legally "dissolved", ending federal services and leading to economic hardship. Some "terminated" tribes have since managed to regain federal recognition. While this policy was in effect, 133 bills were introduced in Congress to permit the transfer of trust land ownership from Indians to non-Indians.

tom-tom - an insulting and improper term for drum.

Tonto - the fictional sidekick of the Lone Ranger and a degrading media characterization of an American Indian, disdained for his lack of sophistication, subservience and ugly pidgin English; (slang) today, an Indian who prefers to fraternize with whites. In Spanish, "Tonto" means "fool."

totemism - a special ritual relationship between social groups or individuals and a special animal, in which the totemic animal is either ancestral or believed to have aided one's ancestors. The animal then becomes a powerful spiritual symbol for that individual, family, or clan.

totem poles - carved wooden poles up to 60 feet tall, erected by Northwest Coast tribes during potlatch ceremonies. Often used as house posts or to mark funerary remains, they are adorned with colorful figures and symbols depicting mythological events, proclaiming status, or tracing historical events of a family or owner through depiction of totemic animals. Today, totem pole carving is an honored and well-paid skill. The phrase "low man on the totem pole" has no basis in Indian tradition.

traditionals - American Indians who live according to many or all aspects of their native culture, choosing to honor their ethnic heritage.

Trail of Broken Treaties - to draw attention to Indian issues, eight Indian organizations formed a car caravan four miles long, arriving in Washington D.C. on November 3, 1971, just before election day. The group presented a twenty-point proposal regarding restoration of treaty rights. Frustrated, they occupied the Bureau of Indian Affairs building for five days.

Trail of Tears - In 1838, 13,000 Cherokees, Choctaws, and Chickasas were rounded up in the eastern United States and imprisoned in Tennessee by the United States Army. In October, they and members of the other Five Civilized Tribes began a forced journey of 800 miles by wagon, horseback and on foot to Indian Territory in Oklahoma. By the end of the six-month winter journey, one out of four had died from exposure, starvation, disease, and abuse.

treaty - a formal agreement between two nations regarding trade, boundaries, alliance, etc. The United States government, often in exchange for huge tracts of land, agreed to provide services (as opposed to welfare) to treaty tribes. The United States government's failure to comply with its own treaties is legend, and Congress terminated treaty-making with Indians in 1871. Modern Indians have found that treaty rights may be reaffirmed in courtrooms, and few non-Indian Americans understand that many treaties are still active law. Originals of all treaties are maintained in the Diplomatic, Legal, and Fiscal Records Division, National Archives and Records Service, 8th Street and Pennsylvania Avenue N.W., Washington,

GLOSSARY

D.C. 20408. Photocopies are available on request.

Treaty of Fort Laramie (1868) - signed by Red Cloud (Oglala) and several other Plains tribal leaders with General William Tecumseh Sherman, the treaty surrendered 30 million acres of land from the Crow to the United States government. The treaty read, in part, "No treaty for the cession of any portion or part of the reservation herein described . . . shall be of any validity or force . . . unless executed and signed by at least three- fourths of all the adult male Indians, occupying or interested in the same." Treaty terms were subsequently ignored by the government. In 1889 President Harrison, unable to convince the Lakota to part with another 9 million acres of their land, declared the Great Sioux Reservation dissolved and created seven smaller reservations. The remaining land was turned over to the new states of North and South Dakota. (Another, 1851 Fort Laramie Treaty formalized tribal land boundaries.)

tribal council - the governing body of most reservations, made up of councilmen elected by adult tribal members and a separately elected tribal chairman.

tribe - a group of persons, families, or bands sharing kinship, territory, culture and/or history. Indian tribes often refer to themselves as nations in recognition of their political emergence.

trust lands - Indian lands protected by the United States government and state governments that are not true reservations. Trust-status tribes are federally recognized, entitled to federal services and the protection of self-government and any trust property.

urban Indians - Indians living in cities.

vanishing American - The title of a Zane Grey story, two films, and an irreverent phrase used in reference to American Indians. Recent population figures reveal that Indians are the fastest growing segment of the United States population.

vision quest - a practice most common among plains tribes, the seeking of contact with spiritual forces, usually through some form of personal deprivation such as remaining in the elements alone for an extended period. Through the vision quest, an individual will receive signs, visions or dreams providing guidance or protection, usually for a rite of passage such as from childhood to adulthood.

warbonnet - a ceremonial headdress with many feathers, a mark of valor worn by the small percentage of western Indians who earn them.

warpaint - paint applied by some tribal warriors to their faces and bodies before going to war. Believed to ward off harm and to evoke fear in enemies.

warpath - the path or course taken by American Indians on a warlike expedition. In popular literature, an inaccurate and disparaging reference to violent or short-tempered tendencies.

warrior society - a prestige society with special rituals and clothing most common among Plains Indians, made up of warriors. Also called soldier society or military society.

wild Indians - the sensationalist and derogatory terms "wild" and "savage" were often used in 1800's media campaigns with political agendas. In reality, Indians fought bravely to protect their homelands.

Wounded Knee - South Dakota site at which, on 29 December 1890, a band of Lakota surrendered to a detachment of the Seventh Cavalry sent out by General Miles two weeks after Sitting Bull was killed by Indian police. Fearing that the ghost dance cult, a reaction to White domination that promoted spirituality over confrontation, would incite an uprising among the Lakota, the cavalry then massacred hundreds of Indians, many subsequently mutilated, including unarmed women and children. Twenty Calvary soldiers received a Congressional Medal of Honor for their involvement. General Miles later repudiated the action as "most reprehensible, most unjustifiable and worthy of the severest condemnation." The last battle of the Sioux wars.

GLOSSARY

In 1973 a group of AIM members and sympathizers illegally occupied the village of Wounded Knee on the Pine Ridge Reservation as an act of protest. They came under siege by the FBI and elements of the United States military out of uniform, who fired tens of thousands of rounds into the area. The siege ended after 69 days and two deaths. Members of the reservation largely decried the act, instigated by outsiders, and have faced a backlash from area residents.

BIBLIOGRAPHY

All American Indian issues, concerns, traditions, and history cannot be developed in this short space, this bibliography provides sources for further research. The following articles and books are written by Indian writers and non-Indian writers with a sensitivity to Native peoples.

Allen, Paula Gunn. "Beloved Women; Lesbians in American Indian Culture."*Conditions* 7. 1981; 67-87.

—-. *The Sacred Hoop*. Beacon Press, 1987.

Bataille, Gretchen M., and Kathleen Mullen Sands. *American Indian Women*. University of Nebraska Press, 1984.

—- and Charles L. P. Silet, eds. *The Pretend Indians*, "Images of Native Americans in the Movies." University of Iowa Press, 1980.

Blue Cloud, Peter. *Alcatraz Is Not An Island*, "By Indians of All Tribes."Wingbow Press, 1972.

Brown, Dee. *Bury My Heart at Wounded Knee*. Washington Square Press, 1984.

—-. *Creek Mary's Blood*. Holt, Rhinehart, and Winston, 1980.

Burnette, Robert and John Koster. *The Road To Wounded Knee*. Bantam, 1974.

Cahn, Edgar, ed. *Our Brother's Keeper; The Indian in White America*. New Community Press, 1969.

Campbell, Maria. *People of the Buffalo*. Salem House Publishing.

—-. *Riel's People*. Salem House Publishing.

Costo, Rupert and Jeannette Henry. *Indian Treaties*, "Two Centuries of Dishonor." The Indian History Press, 1977.

Cohen, Felix S. *Handbook of Federal Indian Law, with Reference Tables and Index*. Washington D.C., U.S. Government Printing Office, 1942. Reprint, Albuquerque: University of New Mexico Press, 1971.

Deloria, Vine, Jr. *Behind the Trail of Broken Treaties*. University of Texas Press, 1985.

—-. *Custer Died for Your Sins*. Avon Books, 1970.

—-. *God Is Red*. Dell Publishing Co., 1983.

—-. *We Talk, You Listen*. Dell Publishing Co., 1970.

—-. and Clifford M. Lytle. *American Indians, American Justice*. University of Texas Press, 1983.

—-. *The Nations Within*. Pantheon Press, 1984.

Densmore, Frances. *Chippewa Customs*. Minnesota Historical Society, 1979.

Foreman, Carolyn Thomas. *Indian Women Chiefs*. Zenger Publishing, 1976.

"From One Sovereign People to Another." *National Geographic*. Sept. 1987: 370-373.

Giago, Tim. *The Aboriginal Sin*. American Indian Historian Press, San Francisco, 1978.

—-. *Notes from Indian Country*. American Indian Historian Press, San Francisco, 1984.

Grahn, Judy *Another Mother Tongue*. Beacon Press, 1984.

Henry, Jeanette. *The American Indian Reader*. The Indian Historian Press, 1973.

BIBLIOGRAPHY

Hirschfelder, A.B. *American Indian Stereotypes in the World of Children*. Scarecrow Press, 1982.

Horsefly, G. P. *The History of the True People, The Cherokee People*. Rich Smith Publishers, 1980.

Howard, Helen Addison. *Saga of Chief Joseph*. University of Nebraska Press, 1978.

Iverson, Peter. *The Plains Indians of the Twentieth Century*. University of Oklahoma Press, 1985.

Kidwell, Clara Sue. "The Power of Women in Three American Indian Societies." *Journal of Ethnic Studies* 6. 1979: 113-21.

Klein, Barry. *Reference Encyclopedia of the American Indian*, 5th ed. Todd Publications, 1990.

Kohl, Johan Georg. *Kitchi-Gami; Life Among the Lake Superior Ojibway*. St. Paul: The Minnesota Historical Society, 1985.

LaDuke, Winona. "In Honor of Women Warriors." *off our backs* II. February 1981: 3-4.

Lakota Times, Native American Publishing — Volume 1 through 11.

Medicine, Bea. "The Anthropologist as the Indian's Image Maker." *Indian Historian* 4. Fall 1971: 27-29.

—. *The Native American Woman*, "A Perspective." National Educational Laboratory Publishing, 1978.

O'Brien, Sharon. American Indian Triban Governments. University of Oklahoma Press, Norman & London, 1989.

Ortiz, Simon. *Song, Poetry and Language—Expression and Perception*. Adobe Press, 1977.

Pacosz, Christina V. *Notes From the Red Zone*. Seal Pr. Feminist, 1983.

Porter, Frank W. III, ed. *Indians of North America Series*. 53 vols. Chelsea House Publishers, 1987.

Stedman, R. W. *Shadows of the Indian; Stereotypes in American Culture*. University of Oklahoma Press, 1982.

Steiner, Stan. *The New Indians*. Delta, 1974.

—. *The Vanishing White Man*. University of Oklahoma Press, 1987.

Stensland, Anna Lee. "American Indian Culture; Promises, Problems, and Possibilities." *English Journal* 60. Dec. 1971: 1195-1200.

Sullivan, Elizabeth. *Indian Legends of the Trail of Tears and Other Creek Stories*. Tulsa, OK: Giant Services, 1974.

Szasz, Margaret Connell. "The Road to Self-Determination Since 1928." *Education and the American Indian*. University of New Mexico Press, 1974.

Underhill, Ruth. *Red Man's America*. University of Chicago Press, 1953.

Vizenor, Gerald. *Earthdivers*. University of Minnesota Press, 1981.

—. *The People Named the Chippewa*. University of Minnesota Press, 1984.

—. *Wordarrows*. University of Minnesota Press, 1978.

"Voices of the People." *Voices from Wounded Knee*. Mohawk Nation, 1974.

Wauneka, Annie D. "The Dilemma for Indian Women." *Wassaja* 4. Sept. 1976; 8.

Witt, Shirley Hill. "The Brave-Hearted Women." *Akwesasne Notes* 8. Early Summer, 1976: 16-17.

Zimmerman, Bill. *Airlift To Wounded Knee*. Swallow Press, 1976

Zitkala Sa. *Old Indian Legends*. University of Nebraska, 1985.